MARKING
TIME

MARKING TIME

Letters from Jean Harris to Shana Alexander

A ROBERT STEWART BOOK

CHARLES SCRIBNER'S SONS · NEW YORK

MAXWELL MACMILLAN CANADA TORONTO

MAXWELL MACMILLAN INTERNATIONAL

NEW YORK OXFORD SINGAPORE SYDNEY

Charles Scribner's Sons
Macmillan Publishing Company
866 Third Avenue
New York, NY 10022

Maxwell Macmillan Canada, Inc.
1200 Eglinton Avenue East,
Suite 200
Don Mills, Ontario M3C 3N1

Macmillan Publishing Company is part of the Maxwell Communication Group of Companies.

Library of Congress Cataloging-in-Publication Data
Harris, Jean (Jean Struven)
   Marking Time: letters from Jean Harris to Shana
Alexander.
      p. cm.
   "A Robert Stewart book."
   Includes index.
   ISBN 0-684-19367-1
   1. Harris, Jean (Jean Struven)—Correspondence. 2. Alexander,
Shana—Correspondence. 3. Criminals—United States—Correspondence.
I. Alexander, Shana. II. Title.
HV6248.H183A4   1991
365'.6'092—dc20
[B]   91-13799

Macmillan Books are available at special discounts for bulk purchases for sales promotions, premiums, fund-raising, or educational use. For details, contact:
Special Sales Director
Macmillan Publishing Company
866 Third Avenue
New York, NY 10022

10 9 8 7 6 5 4 3 2 1

PRINTED IN THE UNITED STATES OF AMERICA

The frame through which I viewed the world changed too. Greater than scene, I came to see, is situation. Greater than situation is implication. Greater than all of these is a single, entire human being who will never be confined in any frame.

Eudora Welty
One Writer's Beginnings

CONTENTS

PREFACE

I began my prison life writing long Dear All letters to my family, but that lasted only a year or so. They all had a way of sounding like the letters I wrote as a child to my grandparents. "Dear Ahma and Papa, How are you? I am fine." I gave them up and now we visit by phone or in person whenever my sisters and brother, nieces and nephews, come east. My sons, Jim and David, are blessedly nearby, so they come to visit frequently. My letter writing, with the exception of an occasional irate letter to the *New York Times* to keep my adrenaline flowing, a letter to the First Lady, a letter seeking clemency, and a few other odds and ends, consists almost exclusively of brief thank-you notes to the many kind friends and strangers who write to express concern for me and ask what they can do to help.

But then there's Shana. Shana is different. She is that rare friend to whom one can tell all and her responses will make sense—to me. I write to Shana Alexander.

In some ways we're very much alike, Shana and I. Our class pictures from high school look enough alike to be interchangeable. We both look so pure, so earnest. We don't particularly look alike today. While our personalities have some likenesses, in some ways we're quite different. Shana is far more worldly than I, having grown up in New York and California in a home where Mother was a movie critic and Father wrote music. He wrote "Ain't She Sweet?" for Shana when she was born. He wrote "Happy Days Are Here Again" to cheer up the country during the Depression, and many other well-known songs in between. She could hear George Gershwin and other musical giants at the living room piano when she had been tucked into bed. I could hear my mother and her friends downstairs at the piano playing all the same tunes—after they were published. We remember a lot of the same music and lyrics. That in itself is a bond.

Shana has had many more lovers than I—many is anything more than one. But like me, only one true love. In spite of the worldliness, however, I think in many ways she is as naive as I am. She can still be genuinely shocked, even if she usually follows what's shocking with a funny or world-weary remark. Her sense of humor is sharp, even biting, and she uses it about herself at least as often as about others.

Shana is far more intellectual than I. She reads and enjoys much more poetry, and her writing, which is very good, is laced with literary allusions I wish I could match. I've read all of her books except the one about me, *Very Much a Lady*. It doesn't tempt me. I haven't read any other books about me, either. In her case, I value the friendship too much to put it to such an unnecessary test.

Our friendship began in a courtroom in some kind of pre-hearing before my actual trial began. Shana smiled at me in a rather shy, kind way, and I smiled back. Later, I would see her looking at me in another courtroom, her eyes saying, I know. I know. I know what it is to love. I know what it is to trust. I know what it is to ache from both.

We met formally in my lawyer's office and began to chat. Both of us can find humor even in the midst of tragedy. That's the only logical explanation of why we're both still alive and reasonably sane. For reasons I can't quite recall or explain, soon after we met I began to call her occasionally when the hurt and the tragedy of my life became more than I could bear alone. It is a thing quite out of character for me to do, but I did it nonetheless and after the first few times had no qualms about it at all.

It wasn't a very kind thing to do, motivated, I'm afraid, by not wanting to burden my family, by not wanting them to know what kind of hell I was going through. Shana could listen and go on with her life. A call to one of my sisters would generate phone calls to everyone else in the family and, worst of all, upset my mother. Shana was always kind and always assured me I hadn't interrupted or awakened her, even the occasional times when I called her in the middle of the night.

She's a good listener and a good understander. She thinks more deeply about people and about herself than I do. Ninety-nine percent of what I think about, 99 percent of what I cry about, has nothing to do with me intimately. It has to do with ideas and principles and other people. Shana rushes in where angels fear to tread, wonders more deeply about why people do as they do, herself included. The result is, I think, she suffers more than I do, and I cannot be the balm for her that she is for me. When I am suffering, she is the first to hear about it. My only gift to her is trust. One of her many gifts to me is compassion.

Today our infrequent visits in person take place in the prison Visiting Room. Our frequent visits are by phone and by letter. I can call her. She can't call me. I can only call collect, which bothers me, but not so much that I don't call. Her notes are two or three lines long and accompany my favorite kind of apple soap or a book she thinks I will enjoy. My letters to her are all different lengths. Some, I find on looking back, are very long, written when I needed someone to share the ramblings of a mind spilling over with caring or high dudgeon or even low dudgeon. Some are only a few lines long, usually written to share my delight in the random wisdom one hears in here from time to time or to take the blows of my anger at the meanness and stupidity that are the constant drip, drip, drip of prison.

The letters to, and talks with, Shana have been my steam vent for ten years and, just as often, my opportunity to express things of concern to me that many would be quick to suggest I don't know anything about. Poised as I am on the edge of seventy, I was long ago programmed to believe the world snickers at a woman who questions things much beyond her own parlor. But prison isn't the best place to exchange recipes and dust the piano. The only positive thing about it for me has been the opportunity to read and consider things that might have slipped by me outside while I dusted the piano.

The letters included here cover the months from January 1989 through February 1991, roughly the two years between Governor Cuomo's second and third refusal to grant me clemency. While I have never before used anything as personal as my letters themselves, much of what I wrote or talked about with Shana before 1989 has found its way into my earlier books. These letters open a small window on a women's prison and a woman's mind in the New York gulag.

Each letter is the rung of a ladder that keeps my head above the frustrations that lead to heart attacks and strokes, at the very least above boredom, depression, and that most unforgivable thing of all, giving up. The result is a picture of prison life, as told by one woman to another woman. It is a reflection, of course, of my character and its flaws as well as the character and flaws of a prison system. So be it.

Some of the letters reflect enough disgust and bitterness to surprise even me, not bitterness because I am here so much as bitterness at the waste and the contempt I feel for it. Overt, gratuitous nastiness or stupidity inflicted upon me by a person in a blue uniform causes a quick chemical reaction within me. In an instant, my mouth goes absolutely dry, which may be God's way of saving me, since it's hard to talk without a little spit and it's usually my mouth that causes my biggest problems.

I read somewhere that "the glory of God is man fully functioning." If true, that makes prison the Antichrist. No one functions fully in prison. No one is required to or even allowed to. Quite the contrary, one is quickly swallowed up by the tiresome, the useless, and the absurd. To function fully is a constant battle between you and the system. To speak the truth is considered arrogance. To speak logic is to be considered a fool or at best a misfit.

Shana makes me go on believing in the reality of me even when the little people, the very little people who suspect they own me, keep picking away, trying to make the essence of me disappear. In spite of their assiduous efforts in that pursuit, I still exist. Much like the old Descartes chestnut, "I think, therefore I am."

As for whether the falling tree in the forest makes a sound if there's no one there to hear it, I simply don't worry about it anymore. The noise of this old tree is heard by one listener, and that's all that's needed to obviate the question, to give the sound reality. I don't relish the comparison of myself to a falling tree, but a case can be made, and God knows, the forest is real and dense. Happily for me, there is someone nearby who listens as branches sway in the wind and even crack and break. This book is for her.

Marking Time

Dear Shana,

A letter arrived from the Clemency Bureau today. "After a careful review of your case it has been determined that there is insufficient basis to warrant the exercise of the Governor's clemency powers . . . such action is taken only in the most compelling circumstances."

It will be another year before I can ask again and then another year of waiting before I receive an answer. The press was given the decision on New Year's Eve, and the Superintendent then gave it to me. In case you might otherwise forget, you are always turned down on Christmas Eve or New Year's Eve. Jolly good idea, what?

The whole process of telling us we are denied (there were three women being considered this year) is treated a little like a death in the family, with hushed voices and sad faces. It's a rotten job for the Superintendent, especially since she had supported all three of us. After being told, we were asked if we wanted to go in to the Superintendent's boardroom for a few minutes to recover our composure. Having not lost my composure, I declined the offer.

1

David had come for a visit and left only moments before I was called down. He heard the news on his car radio and was devastated. Poor guy, he was so hopeful. When your judge, jury foreman, other jury members, world-respected pathologists and criminologists, newspaper editors, and thousands of private citizens plead in your behalf, one dares to hope. But for now there is no hope.

Fondly,
Jean

Sunday, February 5, 1989

My dear Shana,

It's Kathy's special day,* and I didn't remember it until I talked with Michael. Two years can go by so quickly or take forever. How easy it is for strangers in her life to go on with their living and all their self-centered concerns. How totally impossible for you, her mother, ever to forget the day, the moment, she died. I believe beyond any doubt that losing one's child is the ultimate tragedy and one I cannot imagine enduring. In the natural course of events, I trust I won't have to.

Death is something I rarely think about; whether that's wisdom or escapism, I can't say. It isn't complicated in my mind's eye, simply the coming of eternal and blessed peace, relief from all the things one cannot understand. I think that is what Kathy was seeking. That is what I believe she found. Having come so close to suicide myself and failed to meet it only by the merest chance, I know it isn't something one does to get even with the world or anyone in it. It is simply the

---

*Kathy, Shana's daughter, committed suicide on February 5, 1987.

end of endurance, and what troubles each of us only we alone can know.

I can't imagine how heavily the day weighs on you, how much you miss her, how constantly you ask yourself, "What more could I have done? Could I have made the difference?" And probably nothing will ever convince you it was out of your hands. I wish that I could convince you, because I believe it. I believe, too, Kathy is at peace and wishes peace for you. And so, dear Shana, do I—

With love,
Jean

February 11, 1989

Dear Shana,

It's the middle of the night, and I am sitting in the midst of total chaos. I moved to 114C, the Honor Floor, this evening, dragging all my worldly possessions with me—in five trips from about two city blocks away, up and down six flights of stairs each trip. Five women on 112A had offered to help me, so we loaded up and could easily have made the move in two trips. But the CO [corrections officer] at the bottom of the first four flights said, "Oh, no! You can go right back upstairs. Only one person can help you. You'll have to carry the rest yourself." The fact that she was talking to a sixty-six-year-old woman with a bum heart was of no concern to her. "You don't get special privileges, you know. You're just like everyone else."

I wonder how many times I've heard that during all these years, always from a woman, never a man. I wonder why they are the truly vicious ones. The few really unpleasant male guards aren't vicious so much as stupid.

My new cell is smaller than all but three other cells on the floor of sixty. Two larger ones are standing empty as I write this. I asked if I could move to one of them. The CO called the sergeant, and the answer came back "She takes the small one or she doesn't move up." The simple decency and impartiality of those who rule the prison are always reassuring. At least this is away from the mobs of cockroaches I've lived with for the past two years. I've grown accustomed to sleeping with my light on. That way, if I wake in the middle of the night and need a light, there aren't twenty or thirty roaches racing for cover.

February 13, 1989

Dear Shana

I awoke my first morning on the Honor Floor to a threat from a short, blond CO telling me if I'm not standing tomorrow when she calls the 6:00 A.M. count, she will write me a Charge Sheet. They may arrange to have me thrown off the floor before I've even unpacked. I finally went to sleep about 4:00 A.M. I must have been in a dead sleep when she called the count. I didn't stand up because I didn't hear her call. I suggested she might call louder. No, she couldn't. I suggested she might knock on my door. "You don't get special privileges. I don't knock on other doors. I don't knock on yours. You're just like everyone else, you know." She made it quite clear that, awake or asleep, I'd better damned well be standing when she comes around tomorrow. I've asked my next-door neighbor to please knock on the wall the minute she hears the woman approach. It's not a good beginning. I'm afraid I will never be an admirable inmate, if that is Bedford's notion of

4

an admirable one. Brownnosing is the furthest thing from my style, and blurting out my very honest opinion is the kiss of death, outside as well as inside. But to compromise either of those two deadly qualities doesn't tempt me at all—and so one pays the price.

Love,
Just Like Anyone Else

February 15, 1989

Dear Shana,

Did you happen to notice that B.H.C.F. [Bedford Hills Correctional Facility] hit the Op-Ed page last week? Young Robert Kennedy lives in the neighborhood and seems to be annoyed that the prison's raw sewage is slopping over into the neighborhood water supply. This in spite of over six thousand citations for violations. It's quite convenient to be the State. Apparently you can get away with things the State itself would penalize a private institution for doing.

Obviously, there's a serious sewage problem here. I've seen raw sewage backing up in 112 Lobby more than once, and that's only a small part of the problem. The plant is old and inadequate since the number of inmates doubled. Moreover, the women exacerbate the problem by flushing anything from plastic cups to whole blankets down the toilets, out of spite, ignorance, or frustration, I don't know which. Added to that, hundreds of thousands of gallons of water are wasted for want of washers on spigots or want of other simple maintenance parts. On two different floors I have seen water flowing full force into a sink for over a year before it was fixed. There are inmates quite capable of making many of the repairs, but they aren't allowed the necessary tools. An outdoor faucet in back of Building 14 gushed full force for over two years before it was turned off.

For months now we've been permitted one five-minute shower every other night. For a while, the shower rooms were kept locked. The CO on duty unlocked the door to let you in, timed you, unlocked the door to let you out and the next woman in. We all knew that wouldn't go on for long, because it required too much time and energy on the CO's part, all that getting up and sitting back down again. Besides, most of them don't give a small damn how long we shower. See no evil, hear no evil, speak no evil. It's easier.

The CO on duty is often a man, and he isn't about to go into the shower room to drag anyone out if she chooses to take a fifteen-minute shower instead of a five-minute one. They don't even check the women who take showers A.M. and P.M. seven days a week.

To save more water, we have also been forbidden to use the washers and dryers on each living unit. We can either wash everything by hand or send it to the prison laundry, a calculated risk at best. Things must be sent in small fishnet bags in which they are both washed and dried. By the time we get them back, they are scrunched up in such a tiny, wrinkled mess you have to wet them again and hang them up dripping wet to get the wrinkles out enough to be able to iron them. At the moment, there is one iron for sixty women. I stand at the door at six-thirty and make a run for it as soon as the doors are unlocked. Washing everything by hand uses more water than the machines do, but the administration insists this is not so. People who run prisons, I find, do not like to be confused by the obvious.

Good night,
Jean

February 23, 1989

Dear Shana,

The best thing about the Honor Floor is that it is much the cleanest and brightest housing unit. Furthermore, shouting obscenities is definitely frowned upon. The Recreation Room has louvered windows on three sides and is a large, pleasant place to eat or to work. For two years on 112A I ate every meal alone in my cell—cereal, toast, fruit, soup heated in my hot pot, whatever, anything to avoid the noise, the pushing and shoving in the hallway to the dining room, and the ugly, ugly language that are all a part of standing in line to be fed here.

For the first time in nine years I have found two pleasant companions to eat dinner with in the Rec. We take turns supplying food. There's a small kitchen on each housing unit, and somehow between thirty and fifty women use it. Less than a fourth of the women go regularly to prison meals. There are sixty women on this floor, and some days only three or four women go down to the prison dining room. The food isn't bad, but the ambience, which is far too grand a word for what's down there, is unpleasant in the extreme. The last time I went down to eat, tempted by a baked potato, Carole took one side of the table and Cookie took the other and banged it hard three times on the floor to dislodge the cockroaches that live underneath. "Rather have 'em on the floor than in my lap," Cookie said. The absence of cockroaches on the Honor Floor is like a breath of spring. I still cringe when I mistake a shadow for a roach. There are some, of course, but nothing like other floors and nothing like the prison dining room. On 112A we took our lockboxes to the shower room on a regular basis, filled the tub with hot water, and plunged the lockbox into it to dislodge this week's or this month's crop of bugs. Needless to say, no one takes a bath. There's something about sharing a tub in an institution where herpes, gonorrhea, syphilis, and TB are on the rise and one in five test

7

positive for the AIDS virus that quenches one's desire for a nice hot bath.

For me the best things about the Honor Floor are the windows in the Recreation Room. A close second is the steam exhaust pipe right outside my window. It whooshes regularly all night long, a breathing-in kind of sound, and then, *whoosh*, like a wave breaking on the shore and then receding. I go to sleep pretending it's the sound of the waves on Lake Erie and I'm back at the cottage again.

Love,
Jean

March 8, 1989

Dear Shana,

I'm still teaching the young mothers in our nursery "The Red Cross Parenting Course: The Infant from Birth to Two," but now we're revving up to start still another parenting course. At the moment it's to be called Intensive Parenting, a poor name, I think, but I haven't convinced anyone else that it is. There will be twenty inmate-students in it who must be able to read and write English. The class will meet five afternoons a week from one-fifteen to three-fifteen. It will last for three months and be team taught by staff members, inmates, and outside experts. The first month will concentrate on student self-esteem, without which it is difficult to be an effective parent. The next six weeks will cover the child's development from birth to early adolescence. The last two weeks will cover family relationships. There will be extensive use of films throughout, the women will keep a journal, and there will be daily selected readings, not a text. I will be teaching the parts on infancy, toddlers, and elementary-school children.

It's fascinating what a popular word, even an overused word, "parenting" has become. I had never heard the word until I came to prison. That was almost nine years ago. I'm older and if not wiser at least better informed. I still don't like the word, but I acknowledge the usefulness of it and the sad fact that a growing number of people in this country who give birth to children don't do much to help them grow up and lack entirely an understanding of what their role is meant to be.

I'll call you Saturday.

Love,
Jean

March 12, 1989

Dear Shana,

It's Sunday, and I have a 10:00 A.M. appointment to see a psychiatrist, who will ask me, "Well, how's everything?" and then not listen, even if I give an answer. The cost of taking 75 mg. of Tofranil a day is to see a psychiatrist on a regular basis, even though seeing him is as useful as falling down stairs. Perhaps it's lack of character or intestinal fortitude or that greatest crime of all, "lack of self-esteem," that keeps me thinking I cannot go this Little House of Bethlehem all alone. There are times when I feel very tall and others when I feel like something squashed on the pavement. I need that little brown pill, even if it's only sugar and water, to make me think I have a link to sanity.

I have weathered nine years in this place, where good is bad and black is white and decency and truth are held laughable. Whether I could have done it without the little brown pill, I don't know. It is called an antidepressant. Next to having a stroke in this unspeakable place, losing my mind is the biggest threat. I think I still have a firm grasp on reality in spite of the fact that truth skirts the edges in here.

If humans who endlessly slop dirty water up and down the same area were what this country needed, we would be sending useful citizens out of this ridiculously overfenced pen. Sad to say, this is not the case. While the country needs well-educated, well-trained people with insight and logic, courageous enough to say the emperor hasn't any pants on, we send out addicted women whose contribution to society may be seven uneducable children, made that way through no fault of their own, who will carry on Mother's cultural habits while the bleeding hearts of the world insist one person's culture is just as good as anyone else's.

Perhaps, all lined up in front of God, one culture may be judged as good as another, but when you move from one environment to another, want the fruits of that new environment, and insist upon bringing the old culture with you, it can be like an albatross around your neck. I don't mean songs and stories and dances and things that enrich any culture, but accepted rules of a society and the way we raise children. I'm sure God would make a very strong case that "I ain't been had no" is just as acceptable to him as "I haven't had any," but if you want what is admired in the new environment, you can't get it, legally, dragging "I ain't been had no" with you.

There have to be standards, arbitrary though they may be, simply because they make life more bearable. Strangely, I find people whose life is most difficult clinging most jealously to what they consider their culture in spite of the role that culture plays in the tragic lives they lead. It's hard to teach in here without coming up against "Who the shit you think you is?" a question I really haven't a good answer for.

Love,
Jean

March 16, 1989

Dear Shana,

Nothing ridiculous surprises me anymore. The White Rabbit himself, hurrying up the hill, insisting he's late for a very important date, would get little more than a raised eyebrow. Take these brief interludes of the week past and try them on for size. . . .

.   .   .

Every day, seven days a week, Connie gets up at 5:45 A.M. to get dressed and deliver all the sign-up sheets for Nurses' Screening. The note posted on her door for the CO's information reads "Door to be opened at 5:45 A.M. seven days a week."

Last Sunday, Connie awoke on her own and noticed it was 5:50 A.M. and the CO still hadn't opened her door. She called him quietly over to her cell and said, "Please open my door. I was supposed to be out at five forty-five."

"Yeah, but this is Sunday," he said.

"The sign says seven days a week."

"I know."

"Isn't Sunday one of the days of the week?"

"Yeah."

"Then why won't you open the door?"

"Because it's Sunday, lady."

He walked back to the bubble and refused to open her door until six-thirty, when all the others were opened. Nobody was going to put anything over on him. . . .

.   .   .

A woman called out to me in 113 Lobby, "Hey, Jean. I been using your name as my aka."*

---

*Also known as.

. . .

Thursday, Virgie passed me on the walkway in front of the hospital, calling out to someone in the doorway, "He who laughs first ain't gonna laugh last, slut."

She had made herself up as a clown, red cheeks circled in black, eyebrows over most of her forehead, eyelashes down to her cheeks.

She acknowledged my presence with "Anybody gives you a hard time, Mrs. Harris, you let me know, I beat the shit outta 'em. I like doing that. I like beating the shit outta people."

. . .

This piece of motherly advice was shouted down the stairwell: "I know where yer comin' from, cuz yer a motherfuckin' Virgo and I am, too. But you ain't gotta have yer ass on yer shoulders just cuz you ain't gettin' yer own way."

Fondly,
Jean
aka Harris
aka 81-G-98

March 20, 1989

Dear Shana,

Intensive Parenting began today. Sister Elaine took the first class, and to the women's delight it was laced with stories from her endless collection. In another life she'd have made a great after-dinner speaker, or even a stand-up comic. Where Sister is there is always laughter and warmth as well as deep thought, total chaos, or a healthy mixture of all four.

"There was a wise old woman," she told the class. "For miles around people knew of her wisdom and traveled many miles to seek her out. Some young people wanted to trick her, to make her look foolish, so they made a plan. 'See this bird,' one said. 'I'll hold it in my hand and ask the old woman whether the bird is alive or dead. If she says, "Dead," I'll open my hand and let the bird fly away. If she says "Alive," I'll squeeze the bird until it's dead.' They went to the woman, and holding out the hand that held the bird, they asked, 'Wise woman, is the bird alive or dead?' The wise woman answered, 'It's in your hands.' " There are many times when I want to say to these young women, "Please, ladies. There's still time left, and it is in your hands." Sister's supply of allegories is endless. Offhand I can't think of one. I'm much too literal, even pedantic, I fear.

Love,
Jean

March 24, 1989

Dear Shana,

You always speak of my teaching in here as though it were something important. I wish you would believe it isn't modesty on my part but simple truth when I tell you what a minor drop in the ocean it is. I've done enough research and reading to prepare for a class at Harvard, but the number of women I work with is small, at best, and then only when there aren't six other places for them to go and there's a place where we can meet.

Many of the women, having raised other children, think there's nothing more to learn about babies. Their knowledge has stopped with what their grandmothers told them or, worse still, what was done to them. The things I try most to impart are an understanding of the remarkable potential and unique-

13

ness of each infant and each infant's need for and right to a loving caregiver.

"Loving" is the key word. Loving and gentle are not the first adjectives these women would choose to describe their own childhoods, but how wonderful if we could help them introduce them into the lives of their own children.

I usually start the class by giving them a copy of a picture from the Sistine Chapel of God reaching out to touch life into Adam. Over the years, while most have never heard of Michelangelo or the Sistine Chapel, they are moved by the picture. They often ask for a copy "For my friend." The whole point is that now *we* must touch life into our children with gentle nurturing. I'm something of a dreamer, but why not?

The importance of infant play is another thing we talk about a lot. It's interesting to me how we've divided "work" and "play" into opposites and then make our own unschooled judgments about what goes in which column.

I tell them briefly of something I read in Grant Fjermedal's book *The Tomorrow Makers*. It's about the young people in great universities who are working in the field of robotics. We still haven't a robot that can think and function as a human being because we still have to program the robot before it does all its wonderful tricks. To arrange for the robot to program itself is, I suppose, the ultimate goal. To achieve it, one young scientist observes, the robot needs the opportunity for

> randomly frolicking . . . kind of wagging its head from side to side and moving it up and down and maybe running around the room for no particular reason. And it's really necessary. This is play. And it's the same reason a young animal has to do a lot of this—to get everything calibrated right. A newborn doesn't know how to use its arms and legs and eyes, and it's just got to play. There's

no need for it to do any particular job, it's being fed and taken care of. But it has to learn how to get all of these things adjusted right. And the only way to do this is to exercise pretty much its full range of things it can do.

The message seems to be that to be truly human we must play, and to make a machine perform as though it were human, it, too, must play. I can't say that my students are deeply moved by this notion, but it blows my mind.

Have you ever asked a group of people, kids or adults, to define "work" and "play"? Sooner or later the lists merge—it's all learning—whether you enjoy it or not is the dividing line.

Love,
Jean

April 4, 1989

Dear Shana,

One of the women panicked when she heard they were about to take urine samples from women on her living unit. If caught with dirty urine, that is, signs of drug use, you can get ninety days in solitary confinement. She stuffed a disinfectant ball up her vagina, thinking it would hide the drugs she had used or at least confuse the tester. Instead, she is in the hospital, painfully burned. Crime breeds a good deal of the tragedy in here, but ignorance takes care of the rest.

Jean

April 15, 1989

Dear Shana,

Department of Incidental Information

A publication of the American Correctional Association tells me that at the turn of the century there will be fifty thousand people over sixty-five imprisoned in this country. This is good news for the federal government and bad news for the states. According to a law passed in time for my sixty-fifth birthday, people in prison cannot receive Social Security, the logic being that since our room and board are provided by the state, we don't deserve the insurance, which, in my case, my employers and I have paid for forty years. The catch is that the state pays my room and board but the federal government keeps the Social Security. The states have tried to sue the federal government for it but to date have lost in court.

The other catch is that while I cannot collect Social Security when I earn nothing, if I should earn anything from my writing, I must continue to pay Social Security, and as a self-employed writer, I pay for both the employer and employee. If the states can put enough old writers in prison for life, it's gravy for the federal government, which can then dip into Social Security with a clear conscience. Maybe this is a way to handle the public debt. At least it's more reasonable than renting out the Stealth Bomber for graduation parties, which someone has suggested.

Prisons may eventually handle the Alzheimer's problem, too. We're handling the drug problem with prisons. We're handling mental illness and homelessness problems with prisons, why not Alzheimer's, too? In time we can return to the charnel houses of the Middle Ages. Just throw all your problems into prison, and *voilà*!—a perfect society.

Love,
Jean

April 20, 1989

Dear Shana,

The mail just came and in it this wonderful quote from the letters of Katherine Mansfield. A thoughtful stranger sent it to me.

Like everything else in life, I mean all suffering . . . we have to find the gift in it. We can't afford to waste such an expenditure of feeling; we have to learn from it.

I think we've both developed a certain talent for searching out "the gift in it." Hooray for us.

Jean

April 28, 1989

Dear Shana,

Thank you for the birthday soap. It has become my favorite luxury in here. Every time I use it, I remind myself if I live long enough to get out of here, I won't be able to afford it. It belongs on that very short list of prison pluses—David reminds me that there is job security in here, too.

I'm feeling particularly springlike today, a combination of the weather and Virginia's garden. I know I've mentioned Virginia to you, a very bright woman who came here a few weeks after I did. We share the distinction of having both been thrown out of Fiske Honor Cottage. I think it's safe to say our alumnae association is one of the most exclusive clubs in the country.

Virginia's garden—actually she has two in progress, but the one I mention is in a small plot next to the old school building. In it are plants she has found growing in lawns or fields all

17

over the facility, hardy plants left over from many years ago, when this was a reformatory and gardens were permitted. She spots a lily of the valley or iris or violet or daffodil and the next thing you know, she's on her knees with a couple of plastic spoons, digging out the stray flower and moving it to the garden, where it will be permitted the luxury of blooming before it is mowed down.

She has put stones around the garden to mark it as a special place, and Mrs. Holohan, the high-school-equivalency teacher and kindred soul who knows that beauty and decency are appropriate even in prison, has asked that the women not pick the flowers but enjoy them together.

When I see Virginia and her plastic spoons working quickly so she won't risk a Charge Sheet for her furtive activity, I think of a summer day more than fifty years ago up at my family's cottage. I was sitting on the floor, trying to teach myself to type—no comments, please. The radio was on, and someone was interviewing Picasso. He was asked, "If you were imprisoned and all your paints and canvasses were taken from you, what would you do?" Picasso answered, "Then I would paint with shit on the walls." I found the answer quite remarkable, my introduction, perhaps, to an indomitable spirit, and I have always remembered it. Virginia, too, is an indomitable spirit.

Love,
Jean

April 30, 1989

Dear Shana,

The state of New York has just signed a new $60 million contract with AT&T to handle prisoners' phone calls in all of the state's fifty-nine prisons. A U.S. district judge had ruled that the public telephone business should be open to all carriers, so twenty different companies put in bids. To put it in AT&T's words, "We had to offer a commission schedule and we were lower than Sprint, MCI, and New York Telephone offered. The way we calculated the commission, however, provided certain benefits to the customer." The benefits amount to something like $9 million to the state this year, which is a percentage of all the calls made. How a "commission schedule" differs from a kickback, I don't know, except one apparently is legal and the other is not.

Wonderful thing, this business of law—and lots of money in it, too, if you just know how to twist its tail.

Love,
Jean

May 5, 1989

Dear Shana,

My Sister Elaine stories always have a kind of warmth to them that makes you feel people are innocent and the world is clean and good in spite of all the bad things we all know about. I wish I could write a book about her, but I couldn't bring in all the facets of her personality so that people could fully appreciate the dichotomy of her earthy humor as well as the devout and deep theological philosophy that propels her through life. Some would find her Rebecca of Sunnybrook Farm. Some would find her "shocking." She always brings warmth and humor with her in to this unfunny place.

Yesterday she was driving four paroled women who live with her at Providence House IV. Glenda was in front. "You know, Sister," she said, "now I'm out and free, I'm gonna start thinkin' about myself, doin' nice things. I'm gonna go places I never been. I'm gonna see the world."

"That sounds exciting," Sister said. "Where do you think you'll go?"

"Well, first thing I'm gonna do is take me to the Bronx Zoo." Charlene, in the backseat, offered encouragement. "Oh, that's a good place to go. You gonna like it. They got a nice class a people goes there." Penny added, "And they got nice restaurants there, too. The food is real good."

Glenda looked happy and expectant. She was really going to see the world. And high time.

Love,
Jean, who has seen
the Bronx Zoo and longs for home

May 10, 1989

Dear Shana,

Sometimes I think it's more blessed to receive than to give. God knows it's harder. You learn about gratitude by giving. You learn about humility by receiving, and in the pecking order of human qualities, I'd probably put humility somewhere before gratitude.

It has been a particularly slow week. I've been trying to read a biography of Queen Victoria, but I find her on the whole boring except for all the pomp and circumstance and the fact that she lived so long and managed to give birth to most of the crowned heads of Europe, or their wives. Up to now we've been great admirers of longevity. If you're old enough, people somehow find you splendid. As more and more people live longer and longer, that will probably change. My timing has always been poor.

Love,
Jean

May 12, 1989

Dear Shana,

Hallelujah! You finally went and got a dog! I'll overlook the fact that it's a stylish, non-dog-pound type. At least it's a dog. In a little while you'll wonder how you survived without it. They're a nuisance, of course, but everything has its price. Wait until you get the vet bills. But oh, a dog is such a loving and dependable character, whatever your own mood may be. They seem to read your moods and react the way you once hoped husbands and children would but rarely did. Every woman who lives in a man's world, and we all still do, should have a dog to sort of complete a man's personality. You can even laugh at them and they don't mind.

Cider, my dear Golden Retriever, was my closest friend and only confidant. It was at least five years in here before I could look at a picture of a dog without being close to tears. I have pictures of them all over the place now, a sign of maturation on my part.

They're amusing, too, dogs, that is, each with its own personality. Some of them are clowns. They make you laugh out loud, and they seem to enjoy the joke, too. Since it's a progressively unfunny world we live in, an amusing, loving companion is something much to be valued. Too bad they can't dance and play bridge; dogs, that is.

Happy days,
Jean

May 26, 1989

Dear Shana,

On Friday afternoons we usually show the Intensive Parenting class a movie, chosen by any one of the teachers for a particular teaching purpose, primarily to help the women see that their sorrows, their strengths and weaknesses, their uncertainties, are universal experiences. Since I came to Bedford, I have wanted the opportunity to introduce the women to some of the great stories to help them appreciate that they are not the pariahs many of them consider themselves to be, that what they feel and what they have experienced make them more like others, not less. I guess the hope was to introduce them to their own humanness.

We've shown them Ibsen's *Doll's House,* which they enjoyed and understood to a point, though Jane Fonda is the last woman on earth to play Nora and helps make it difficult for all of us to relate to Ibsen's groundbreaking feminism. Even with Fonda it's more realistic than much of today's you-can-have-it-all literature.

We've shown Flannery O'Connor's *Displaced Person,* which needs some history background to give it the depth it deserves, a *History of Black English, Gorillas in the Mist, The Kiss of the Spider Woman, A Clockwork Orange* (which I don't understand, either, and am not highly motivated to try to), *The Devil and*

Daniel Webster, The Secret Garden, The Red Pony, Almos' a Man, Lean on Me, and others.

So far, *The Devil and Daniel Webster* elicited the most responses. We talked for a little while about the story of Faust, whom no one had heard of, and Rumpelstiltskin, whom one thought sounded familiar. They liked Daniel Webster's speech in the mock court so much they asked to hear it again. I guess such an articulate and moving plea to forgive us our trespasses is destined for success in here. I told them the movie had been made years ago, when I was their age, and though the story of selling your soul to the devil will never grow old, if they made the movie today, they might choose someone besides Daniel Webster to face off with the devil. "If you were casting the story today, whom would you choose for that role?" Without a moment's hesitation, three women said, "Jesse Jackson."

"How about the devil's choice of jurors?" I asked. "They were all rogues and scoundrels but real figures in history who had in their own ways sold their souls to the devil. Is that the kind of jury you would pick?" Some said they'd have picked good people who hadn't sold their souls. Others disagreed and said the ones who had sold their souls and gone to hell would be more full of regret and more apt to forgive others. One said, "Well, you wouldn't want any lawyers on it, because Jason signed a contract." Several suggested you wouldn't put a lawyer on a list of people who hadn't sold their souls to the devil, anyway.

They made their own lists of jurors good and bad. On the rogue side their first and unanimous choice was "Richard Nixon." They aren't given to paying much attention to the news, but it's hard to have lived in America in the past twenty-five years and not heard of Watergate, so first place on the rogue side went to Nixon. The rest of the list belonged to a mixture of whites and blacks, drug dealers they know, Mafia members, serial killers, the like. The list of good people contained only blacks, among them George Washington Carver, Paul Robeson, Harry Belafonte, Martin Luther King, Sammy Davis, Billie Holiday, and Thurgood Marshall. I love it when they come alive and think and disagree.

Today they came alive all right, with a vengeance, but the only one they disagreed with was me. I showed Steinbeck's *The Pearl*. When it ended, two of the women got up and slammed out of the room, yelling obscenities as they went. "Who the shit you think you are, makin' us sit through all that and then they throw the pearl away? Whole thing was for nothin'. All that story for nothin'. What we watchin' that for?" The second one to leave gave me the distinct impression that she was going to hit me on the way out.

The story, as you may or may not remember, is of a young couple and their baby. They live in a small fishing village where everyone exists from day to day from the men's meager earnings as divers for oysters. The young man finds a beautiful pearl and dreams of buying his wife a pair of shoes with his new wealth and books so his son will learn to read. People try to cheat him out of the pearl's worth, then to steal it. The couple flee from the village into the hills and are pursued by robbers. The man kills one of the robbers and captures the other, but only after his young son has been killed, too. In the last scene the couple return to their village, stand on a cliff overlooking the ocean, and the man, with her tacit consent, throws the pearl back into the sea.

Not one of the women could see any conceivable reason for such insanity. For them everything begins and ends with money or the lack of it. "It was bad enough the baby have to die; then they go and make it all for nothing," one said. "I never watch movies don't have a happy ending," another said. "But that isn't what life is like," I argued. "Maybe they felt the responsibility of the pearl was more than they could handle. Maybe they were happier before they found the pearl." "But they coulda been happier with it." "Now if they have another son he isn't gonna learn to read." "Don't show us any more stories like that. It don't make sense; it just make ya feel bad."

I guess the moral is, if you're going to teach us about humanness, don't bring the stories too close to home.

Love,
Jean

June 5, 1989

Dear Shana,

The *New York Law Journal* has an interesting article today about one *D. Smith* v. *the State of New York*. He was indicted, tried, and found guilty in Westchester of two counts of sodomy and two counts of robbery and sent to prison for two consecutive sentences of 8 ⅓ to 25 years. He sued for wrongful imprisonment under the Unjust Conviction and Imprisonment Act and after six years has won his case, cleared by "clear and convincing evidence" of all four indictments.

The court found "reversible error committed in the prosecuting attorney's questioning of . . . the sex crime investigator," who was "unqualified to give expert testimony"; in "material evidence that was withheld from the defense"; and in "the summation of an apparently overzealous prosecutor" (who would, of course, know the testimony he was pounding home had come from an unqualified witness). The prosecutor? George Bolen.*

Six years of a person's life had gone by before the final finding was made, six years in the life of a person who is now declared totally innocent of the crime that sent him to prison,

---

*The assistant district attorney who prosecuted the Jean Harris case.

six years of life that wouldn't have been wasted if everyone had played fair.

George Bolen's modus operandi has not improved with age.

Sad to say,

Jean

June 11, 1989

Dear Shana,

There's another new memo on the bulletin board. The purpose of this one is "to process visits more efficiently," and it proclaims that henceforth inmates may wear only white blouses or shirts in the Visiting Room, and no jewelry (except wedding bands, of which there are precious few). The blouses may be state or personal. It adds that no diaper bags may be brought into the Visiting Room when women on the nursery bring their babies for visits. And no bottles, no washcloths, and no diapers may be brought in, either! "Diapers and food will be provided." It doesn't say by whom. How this will "process visits more efficiently" beats the hell out of me.

From now on every visit to the Visiting Room will be delayed while the CO in traffic decides whether or not a blouse is white. They'll be drunk with this new power. Did you ever try to match a ball of white yarn? There are hundreds of shades of white. This is grist for little mills.

The jewelry rule springs from the fact that the CO's have to write down what jewelry you wear into the Visiting Room to be sure you don't come back with anything new. Anything gold can of course be used in place of money and be used for drugs. Instead of punishing those who bring in gold illegally, it's far easier to tell every woman she can't wear any more jewelry. This doesn't stop any drug traffic—those intent upon it just stuff the money, gold, or drugs farther up their vaginas and go about their trade. Only those with no intention of bringing in contraband are punished. The others are momentarily inconvenienced.

Nothing serves morale in here more than permitting a woman to look nice for her family and friends, and anyone who thinks morale plays no role in prison, or shouldn't, is not thinking clearly.

Love,
Jean

June 16, 1989

Dear Shana,

Two of the older (fifty-to-sixty-year-old) ladies were having an early-morning chat about something that seems to pervade the institution more and more each day—homosexuality, lesbianism. "It ain't a matter of more education. You don't have to go to no college to know right from wrong. Men sleepin' with men, women sleepin' with women, that's somethin' that come right outta the jaws a hell. It ain't meant to be, tryin' to fit together two things ain't meant to fit. Like that wall plug over there. If the plug ain't built right, it ain't goin' in to that socket, and anybody with a ounce a sense knows it!"

You don't have to read *Our Bodies, Ourselves* to learn the facts of life in here. Just keep your ears open.

Love,
Jean

June 23, 1989

Dear Shana,

Much as I dread every instant of it, I went to the hospital today for another stress test. This was a kind I had never had before, where you ride a bicycle and watch your heart on a TV screen.

We are told about hospital trips only a few hours or even a few minutes before we leave so we will not arrange a prison escape with our dangerous confederates on the outside. One of my seventy-five-year-old friends could easily arrange a road-block on the way to the hospital and with all guns blazing fly me off to a distant island, where I could live out what's left of my life, in splendor, on my vast personal wealth.

My trip began with the usual harassment by whichever armed female CO was going to accompany me. She and the CO driver—there must always be two—make any outside hospital trip a very expensive one for the taxpayer. Strange, sad, how often the taxpayers defeat school bond issues but never, never ask where all the money for prison goes.

There are some very decent female COs who accompany inmates to the hospital. I didn't draw one. CO X approached me, her chains in hand, and immediately announced, "You're not taking that book with you." I had brought a small paper-back with me for what I knew would be hours of waiting. "Take off your watch. Get that hair band off. You can't wear a plastic headband to the hospital. Now get in there and take your clothes off—everything—off."

She took me into a dirty little lavatory and stood there while I stripped. I still didn't remove the headband. "Take off that headband. You're not wearin' no headband to the hospital." "That's ridiculous," I told her. "I've worn this thing every day for nine years, including every time I've gone to the hospital. My hair is thick and falls in my face, and I'm not going to go through a stress test with hair in my face and my mouth."

"Everything off." "Look," I told her, "let's just save everyone's time and cancel the trip." "I'm followin' procedure," she said. "I follow procedure." "Fine," I said. "I certainly can't keep you from following procedure. You can make me take off all my clothes, and you can make me take off the headband. But you can't, by law, make me go to the hospital. So just cancel the trip and save everyone's time."

"Did I say you couldn't wear the headband?" she asked. "Did I say it?" "Yes. You said it three times." "Did I say you couldn't wear it since you said your hair falls in your face? Did I? Did I? So if I didn't say it since then, that means you can wear it, don't it?"

"Fine," I said. "And I need the book, too. A paperback book is permitted to prisoners in the hospital. I am not going to sit for hours with nothing to do."

"All right, all right. I let you take the book, too. But I carry it. I have to carry it."

Once dressed again, I stood while she placed a heavy five-inch leather belt, complete with handcuffs attached, around my waist, then locked on the handcuffs. This way you can maneuver in such a way as to scratch your nose but not your head, which immediately starts to itch. They let me walk to the prison van before they locked on the leg irons. Thus seated in the prison van, with two armed guards to accompany me, I was taken to the hospital for a stress test.

The test is an expensive one to administer. If a private citizen has it, it can cost anywhere from six hundred to a thousand dollars. It wasn't until I was partway through the test, and my heart was not pumping as hard as it should in order to get the needed information from the test that I learned that I should not have taken any heart medication this morning or yesterday, either. But then, if they had told me, I might have figured out that I was going to the hospital and set up the roadblock. The kind young doctor who administered the test said not to worry. It would probably tell them what they needed to know.

When we left, the prison van wouldn't start until a woman drove up beside us and loaned us her jumper cable. I asked why they don't keep jumper cables in prison vans and was told by the CO driving, "No point. They'd just be stolen," and not by inmates. The salary of two COs for at least three hours, some of it overtime, plus the cost of the test was well over twice what the cost of a similar test for normal people would be. There are fifty-three thousand state prisoners in New York State. Imagine the medical costs.

Love,
Jean

June 24, 1989

Dear Shana,

It was graduation day for our first Intensive Parenting class. On the whole, the class went reasonably well, considering how new we all were to the task, students and teachers alike. It's quite possible the teachers learned more than the students, but then, that's often the case.

Graduation consisted of cake and coffee and a certificate that I made and matted for each of them. The morning the certificates were to be given out we were told, "Hold those certificates. The women can't have those; they're framed. Frames are not allowed per directive." They weren't framed, they were matted, and the certificate was glued to the matting; otherwise, they were too flimsy to be saved, and certificates of accomplishment mean a great deal to the women here. They are not only saved but displayed with pride.

These are the moments I wonder why I haven't had a stroke. Instead of coming to the ceremony and cheering the women on, administration was making a federal case over two pieces of paper pasted together. Finally, after hasty diplomatic overtures from Sister Elaine, we were permitted to give out the certificates under the condition that we then collect them immediately after the ceremony and send them out to the families. "They cannot be kept in the institution." The women had no say in the matter. We made them flimsy copies to keep. Some of them had no one to send the original to. So much for self-esteem.

Love,
Jean

June 25, 1989

Dear Shana,

It's Sunday evening and Gloria is talking about the morning church service. "It was beautiful, beautiful. I come back and fall on my knees and tell the Lord what I ain't never told no one. And he ain't never gonna tell nobody. I'm blessed! I am blessed! If I don't never get out of prison, I'm goin' to heaven right from here. Hear it! Hear it! I am goin' to heaven right from here!"

As for me, I would prefer to leave from New Hampshire.

Love,
Jean

June 30, 1989

Dear Shana,

John Kenneth Galbraith gave the commencement address at Smith this spring. His speech was printed in the alumnae bulletin. I'd like to have heard him. He strikes me first as honest, something he gets away with by disguising truth as humor. Simple, bald honesty, I have discovered over the years, is something only special people can carry off and still be invited back.

His subject was "institutional truth," as opposed to "painful reality." That is, widely accepted "truths" that bear little relationship to reality but which better serve the organizations that dominate and guide society, business, and government alike. The subject struck home for me because I have always read, heard, and believed that America spends more money on the education of its young than any other industrialized nation in the world. Now I discover that if the expenses of college and universities are removed and only preschool and primary and secondary school are included, America's public and private spending ties for twelfth place out of sixteen nations! If you count only public spending, we come in fourteenth. Australia and Ireland spend less. Sweden, Switzerland, Norway, Belgium, Denmark, Japan, Canada, West Germany, France, Great Britain, the Netherlands, Italy, spend more. The numbers hold whether measurement is per-pupil expenditure or outlays as a proportion of national income.

In what are make-or-break years in a child's educational as well as emotional and social life, our spending is penurious. America's educational edifice is a pyramid turned upside down. One out of four children who should be in Head Start have facilities to serve them. And these are run by teachers who are disgracefully underpaid (about a third of the starting pay of a prison guard!). By first grade many of our children can barely speak, let alone read. By college, we lead in expenditure, but by then more than half of our young people are no longer concerned. In fact, more than 40 percent of them have quit school before they graduated from high school.

Mr. Galbraith said:

> This is a time of great change in both the socialist and nonsocialist lands. Institutional truth, however, is sadly in conflict with the needed accommodations to that change. . . . I pray that you leave these lovely precincts with a powerful commitment to the old Pulitzer rule—that in all life one should comfort the afflicted, but verily also one should afflict the comfortable, and especially when they are comfortably, contentedly, even happily wrong.

This country still doesn't even have a child care law.

Love,
Jean

July 2, 1989

Dear Shana,

I keep promising myself to write an article entitled "Are You Prepared to Be a Juror?: Is Anyone?" It would take more quiet study time than I ever seem to be able to find.

I have many questions about the jury system, though as a good American one must hasten to say, "Well, it may not be perfect, but it's the best system there is." I don't know enough about other systems of justice to know that for sure. Often when that statement is made, our system is being compared to a kangaroo court or the arrogance of one man who has made himself the whole justice system in a Third World country.

Why can't all jurors take notes? Would the average juror accentuate the irrelevancies and ignore what is substantial?

Is the average citizen qualified to judge between starkly contrasting testimony on corporate law, tax law, biological evidence? For that matter, is the average judge? I've heard some pretty cockeyed decisions by judges in the past few years. Case in point: It was discovered that a prosecutor in Brooklyn who had been trying cases for twenty years had never gotten around to taking his bar exams. Some of the people he had been instrumental in sending to prison asked for new trials. A judge's recent answer? "No. Wrongdoers should not profit from the wrongdoing of others." If you think about that for a while, it becomes less and less logical.

Another day, maybe.

Love,
Jean

July 10, 1989

Dear Shana,

I went down to breakfast this morning, more out of boredom than anything else, though I did hope to get a small box of cereal to take back to my cell. I was standing in line, waiting to be served, when I turned rather suddenly to my right and the woman standing directly in back of me apparently thought I was going to touch her. In an instant, her hand shot out, and she grabbed my arm, digging her nails into my arm as she grabbed. "Don't you touch me, bitch," she yelled. "I kill the bitch who touch me." I was so surprised I drew back quickly, but not before she had left a one-inch gash in my arm. It hurt, but I didn't realize it was bleeding until I looked down and saw blood on the side of my blouse.

I knew the woman. It was Pat, who for years had been on the mental ward but recently had been moved up into regular population. She had had violent mood swings there, from warm and cheerful to black withdrawal, when she sat alone and wouldn't speak. What prompted her move to regular population, God knows. I can think of nothing except someone even sicker needing the cell in West Wing.

After breakfast she was standing at the locked gate as I approached. "Pat," I said, "I didn't mean to frighten you. I'm your friend." "Don't come near me, bitch," she bristled. "Next time you touch me I kill you. You don't touch me 'cause you ain't got the a-thor-i-tee to touch me." A guard finally opened the gate, and I went back to my cell.

Later, sitting here, I tried to imagine the life experiences of a woman ready to kill someone she thought was about to touch her. Maybe it was life experiences; maybe it's only the terrible sickness in her mind. Whichever it is, her mood swings will probably last her lifetime and keep bringing her back to a prison cage.

Love,
Jean

July 11, 1989

Dear Shana,

We're in the middle of our 11th Summer Program for inmate children, when they come to spend the whole visiting day with their mothers, each day for five days, and spend evenings with host families in the Bedford area. We'll have 160 children this summer. The picture is much like the one you saw last summer when you found me jumping rope on the terrace. I'm good for about four hops and that's it. But

I'm a splendid turner. These kids do Double Dutch as easily as you and I walk.

Summertime is when I'm reminded again what different names black youngsters have today from the ones they had two generations ago. I almost wrote one generation ago, but it's two now, isn't it? Age hits one in the face every now and then. The days of Franklin D. Roosevelt Jones are long gone. The children who visit their mothers today have totally different names than their grandmothers and grandfathers had.

A "sh" sound is soft and pleasing to the ear, and it appears in, I believe, a majority of the names we hear today. Perhaps this has its origin in Africa, I can't say. There's Shanice, Elishida, Jashawn, Shannea, Shamara, Shaline, Tosha, Tanisht, Kalisha, Chivanne, Kiesha, Purvish, Rayshonne, Shawntay, Maniecia, Elisha, Shaqua, Sharita, Sha Sha, Chevetter, Shakil, Tanisha. The list is long. Soft sounds, soft names. They are imaginative names, often made up by a mother out of thin air. Some of them are lovely, some are awkward to pronounce and will soon be reduced to nicknames.

Some names without the "sh" sounds show further signs of Africa, bits of the Bible, and a mother's imagination. Deyanira, Leyode, Quatainia, Verquan, Yakima, Lozy, Dadé, Dentriss, Jahma, Tahee, Moleck, Kahien, Edrelie, Jadon, Zulma, Baheen, Makiya, Deltonk, Tenquine, Wazaro, Niquas, Jaborn, Addasiah. A search for roots or the finding of them is reflected in all of them. Sometimes the mother herself is not sure of the spelling and will change it from time to time. They open a whole new range of sounds and declare, "We are African Americans. We have a heritage and a culture all our own. And we are proud . . . at least we are trying to be proud."

Love,
Jean

July 15, 1989

Dear Shana,

The prison guards who come here from Sing Sing or Attica or almost any of the men's prisons tell us, "This place is a country club." Well, just about everything else has been changed since I've been a member of this club; maybe country clubs have changed, too.

In one respect, I know we're alike, country clubs and Bedford, that is. Our annual dues are high. In fact, with the possible exception of a golf club in the middle of Tokyo, Bedford's dues are among the highest of any clubs in the neighborhood, over forty thousand dollars per year, if you count all the carrying charges . . . and that's before you play a round of golf, a set of tennis, or take the family to a Thursday night buffet. Here, of course, we don't have sports and buffets. We run the bills up with medical care and lawsuits. We're a sickly bunch, so it's possible for one member to run her club costs up into six figures, and the lawsuits that are apt to spring from the club's medical care run the dues up even higher. Our medical bills average over a thousand dollars a year more than those of members of other clubs.

Fortunately for Bedford members, most people have to pay their own club dues; the taxpayers pay ours, and they seem so positive about the arrangement they keep insisting the membership be increased. It has more than doubled in the last five years. It's a good thing they feel this way, since few of our members have ever earned $40,000 a year, including me. Working full-time at our club responsibilities, we can earn as much as $7.76 per week, $403 per year, which wouldn't cover a month's caddie fees. Before you turn in your membership here, you could easily be more than half a million dollars in debt. I'm not sure if that's trickle-up or trickle-down economics.

Some of the world's top money men belong to country clubs

outside and share their expertise with the club management to keep the club in the black. Strangely, some of the same men forsake the economic philosophies they live their own lives by and also play roles in the economic insanity that governs clubs like this. We run in the red. In fact, it's sometimes difficult to find a reputable business that will deal with us because we're very slow payers.

There's a different process for joining this country club from those outside. While most are voted into their clubs, it's more accurate to say that we are flushed into ours. Length of memberships vary! Some members stay only a few years and move on; some stay for a lifetime. At other clubs the worst-behaved members are sometimes invited to leave. Here we keep them, and if they do leave, obnoxious as they may be, they can be readmitted again and again. Either our membership committee is less discriminating or the club needs the dues.

And yet we do pick and choose our members. There's a strong preference for poor, sickly, uneducated minorities. On the whole, most country club members are movers and shakers. One reads about them in the *Wall Street Journal* to discover how rich they are and in *Vogue* or *Vanity Fair* to see what their homes look like and what designer clothes they wear. In such clubs there is power. In our club there is powerlessness. Our members live on free-fall, sustained by the empty hope that "what go around come around," and someday "they'll get theirs."

A careful look at our club roster would lead one to suspect that not only is this not a country club; it is public housing for the poor. An easy mistake to make. Some who resign their memberships and leave have nowhere to go that is as nice as this. For them, perhaps, one can accurately say that this is as close to a country club as they may ever come.

The cultural and economic differences between members of your club and the paid staff is probably greater than it is in here. As at all clubs, paid help can run the gamut from excellent to intolerable. The big difference is that at this club the overtly rude or even dishonest employee is rarely fired.

Unlike most country clubs, we're even open on Mondays for member visitors. But after visitors leave there's a fascinating club ritual unique to us. It perpetuates the old club motto *Semper Ignominiae Sumus*, which, translated freely, means "We are always trash." Briefly, the ritual consists of the member removing all her clothes while a staff member examines her and her clothes. The ritual finale ends with the member, naked, squatting and coughing for the staff member. I don't know whether other clubs permit the hired help such license, but then I'm not judging, just asking.

Incidentally, since I mentioned buffets, I should explain that we are especially proud of our economies in the kitchen. Members are fed three meals per day (those that bother to go to meals) on a budget of just under two dollars per day. One fairly salivates thinking of the buffet delights one could conjure up with that kind of money.

I rarely eat in the dining room, not because of the food but because it is sometimes served on trays crusted with yesterday's meals; even when bread and butter or meat are served, a fork is the only utensil provided; wherever you sit, an employee invariably tells you to sit somewhere else, while others, arms folded, legs apart, stand and stare at you as you eat. I have been to six meals in the past two years. That brings my club food bill to about two dollars per year, but it doesn't lower the dues.

There's a strong paternalistic air about this club. It wants to take more care of its members than some members need or want. While many members would be glad to provide their own clothes, and do supply as many as are permitted, the club insists upon giving us some, too. I have taken the minimum of club issue and taken very good care of it, so my (annual) clothes bill probably runs somewhere between twenty and twenty-five dollars. That doesn't reduce the annual dues, either.

For some members, of course, perhaps as high as one-third, the paternalism is wanted and needed. They are the ones who, for mental, physical, or emotional reasons, will never be able to provide for themselves. We have many more of these than the average country club would have, among the dues payers at least.

Oddly enough, it's a club rule here that mothers cannot live with their children. In fact, they can't leave the club grounds for years on end, and sometimes forever. They can't live with their husbands, either, but that's a minor problem because only about 10 percent have husbands and about 2½ percent know where their husbands are.

The high hedge or fancy wrought-iron gates that serve to keep strangers out of most clubs here are twelve-feet high, wired, razor-sharp fences to keep members in. Our members can't nurse a sick child, and if the child is in the hospital, they can't visit her. In fact, they must beg for the privilege of calling the hospital to find out if the child is dead or alive. And they don't always get the privilege.

Our members are very familiar with illness, in themselves and in their children. Many members are scarred where knives or fists have caught their faces, where dirty needles have left deep lesions, or where illness has left them totally devastated. One in five members tests positive for the AIDS virus. What are other clubs doing about that? I wonder. Do you do any blind testing of members, as we do?

Death comes early here, too. Mothers of club members have a habit of dying early of cancer, and their sons, of being shot dead in the streets. This week, on my floor, the body count is three, one nephew, one cousin, one brother. If your child or parents die while you're here, you are allowed to go to the funeral if it isn't out of state, and you go chained hand and foot, dragging your chains behind you like Marley's ghost. If you have to go to the hospital yourself, the chains come, too, which is particularly inconvenient if you are in the final stages of labor.

On the whole, it isn't much fun here in spite of the high dues or any reports to the contrary. One thing I almost forgot—the result of my superannuated condition, I suppose. All sexual liaisons in this club are forbidden, and unless there has been a true revolution in country clubs in the past nine years, this is where our similarities definitely part company. A country club dance with no sex after the music stops, or even while it's going on, is not the country club dance of yesteryear.

Of course, there is some sex here, but it's illicit and illegal, and when you see the areas where it has to take place, even the damp grass on the seventeenth green looks good.

There are those who tell us sexual abstinence is the road to spiritual peace, but it doesn't work that way here. Since the average membership age is twenty-six, spiritual peace often gets short shrift.

There are other little miscellaneous differences in the Bedford Correctional Facility Club—enough so I am left wondering how anyone could call us a country club. But people do. The more I ponder the whole subject, the more I am puzzled how anyone, even a disgruntled taxpayer, could mistake this top-security prison for a country club. But then taxpayers are in a better position to do comparison shopping. I can only suggest that if the comparison is a legitimate one, stop paying your club dues. You've been had.

Love,
One of the ladies of the club

July 20, 1989

Dear Shana,

Webster says a show-off is one "given to pretentious display" and an exhibitionist is "one who desires to make an exhibition of herself." I plead not guilty to both counts, but it is only through the intervention of my friend Babe that I am saved. Without her I would forget more frequently than I do to put up my privacy curtain when changing clothes and be exposed in bra and pants, something not frowned upon by many females I have lived among but an absolute no-no to the women of Bedford Hills Correctional Facility.

It would take nothing more than a few Vassar or Smith girls in here to foster a cause célèbre because of all things our lack of modesty. I definitely shock the ladies in my rather casual use of the privacy curtain, a piece of material held up by Velcro and used when the door is open and you are getting dressed or undressed.

"Oh, Jean, I can see your panties. Put up your curtain, girl. I can see your panties. Ain't she somethin' standin' there like that. Put up your curtain." The voice is Babe's. She is one of my near neighbors and a kind friend. She is thirty years younger than I am, but she takes care of me in a motherly sort of way, scolding me when I leave my watch on the lockbox near the door. "You in prison, girl. You gonna lose that watch you keep leavin' it by the door. You in prison." And constantly reminding me about the curtain.

I was changing my school blouse and slacks so I could wear them another day when Babe caught sight of my "panties." My privacy curtain had fallen, or maybe I hadn't put it up, since I in bra and pants am more covered than any ladies at the beach, and more than some of the ladies at the office, with their third of a yard of material that passes today for a skirt. I grew up in a home with three daughters, went to a girl's prep school and a woman's college, so I've never been able to get up a head of steam about being exposed in bra and pants. The only thing I really object to is having underpants called "panties." It's like calling the rich "well-to-do."

It occurred to me while Babe was doing her best to protect my reputation that in nine years I have never seen a woman in here in bra and pants. It's nothing I've made a particular goal of mine, but when you think of it, a few hours at a college reunion at Smith and you probably would have had at least one gabfest with a few people changing dresses or blouses and no one thinking anything of it, no giggles, no embarrassment. In here, privacy curtains are taken very seriously and usually put up before you change your shoes.

I've never observed a similar fixation in other women. Maybe the rampant homosexuality in here makes the fixation a godsend. Maybe it even explains it. I'm not much of an expert in this field.

Keep your curtain up,
Jean

August 3, 1989

Dear Shana,

I've been reading A. N. Wilson's biography of Tolstoy. What a piece of scholarship! Why is it that interesting men are often such bastards and leave such a path of family misery in their wake? The book left me with much to think about.

Did you know that Tolstoy's favorite book was *David Copperfield*? Dickens had inherited from Rousseau the concept of "original innocence" rather than original sin, and Tolstoy adopted the same conviction. "The children in Dickens are all angels," he wrote. "It is the cruelty or hamfistedness of the grown-ups that corrupts them: the grime of cities, the squalor of workhouses, the absurdity of classrooms." I personally think now, 140 years later, the same strong case could be made, which makes my determination to keep the Children of Bedford Foundation alive and functioning all the stronger. Unfortunately, I do believe a child can be destroyed virtually beyond repair very early. When will it be politically popular to acknowledge this? This country is run by what gets votes, not what builds for the future. Unfortunately, what gets votes are money and power, and little children don't have either.

Edward Banfield wrote, "Class can be defined on the basis of people's behavior toward their own future." If he is right, and I think he is, we have only to see how America fails so many of its little children to place us where we stand on an international social values scale ... somewhere among the lower classes. Jonathan Kozol goes so far as to suggest that we have created of our children a class of "New Untouchables." With 13 million children living in poverty, many without a roof over their heads as well as inadequate food and no medical care, they grow up as children at risk in every sense of the word. We treat them as castaways before they are able to walk and then damn them roundly when they fullfill our own prophecies and become criminals.

You can't live as close to the women and children of Bedford as I do and not be touched by Wilson's observation:

> The vast majority of the human race drifts without record from conception to extinction. Their lives go unrecorded, and it is only theology which might make us suppose that these individual lives have any previous or future existence, or indeed during their palpable existence on earth, that they have any identifiable existence. For most, it is a tale full of sound and fury signifying nothing, but most significant of all, it is a tale which is not told.

I know of no substantive follow-up study of young mothers and their children that has been made since Bedford became a prison in 1933. Some, of course, soon return as parole violators or with a new charge. The rest quickly disappear into the streets of the city and cannot be found, their tale untold.

Jean

August 14, 1989

Dear Shana,

One more memo to add to the endless collection.

Effective Aug. 21st all girls that are called to come to the State Shop will have fifteen minutes from the time the call is placed to get to the shop. You will not be called a second time on the same day and you will have to rewrite for permission to come. After 15 minutes you will be turned away.

Myrtle

Myrtle, until recently, was checkout girl at the Commissary. Now she is in charge of the State Shop. One soon becomes drunk with power here. The State Shop is where you go to get state-issued clothing.

There are some women who do everything when and only when they get damned good and ready. There are others who make every effort to get to places on time and are completely at the mercy of COs, who may or may not remember to tell you you have been called and then may or may not get up promptly to open the doors that stand between you and the place you are supposed to go.

A CO watched me standing at a door for a good five minutes

last week while she deliberately refused to come and open it. Finally, I asked her if she was going to open it. "Ah come when ah come," she responded. Tell me about fifteen-minute deadlines.

Love,
Jean

August 18, 1989

Dear Shana,

I've become a follower of what I'm told Sherlock Holmes called the Doctrine of Discriminating Obliviousness. My brain, without any conscious effort on my part, simply closes the door on things I don't care about or don't wish to hear.

At college I used to be disturbed by the scratching of some-one's pen. Now, though my cell is closest to the kitchen, Rec Room, TV, all the big noisemakers, I rarely hear a sound. I consider this a God-given gift, and it doesn't go unappreci-ated. I'm passing through a look-on-the-bright-side period.

Love,
Little Mary Sunshine

August 20, 1989

Dear Shana,

Louise goes out next week. She was in my Red Cross Infant Course. She came to hug me good-bye. Louise has AIDS. Her baby has AIDS; her husband died of AIDS four months ago. Yesterday her fourteen-year-old son, who lives with her sister, shot and killed his two-year-old cousin. The gun was in the house. He says he didn't know it was loaded. Loaded or unloaded, the fact that a fourteen-year-old would point a gun and shoot toward a two-year-old infant is a pretty good sign he has some serious problems.

Louise hasn't a job. She hasn't a waiting family. She has only two sick children and her own sick body. She must be happily content to die with her baby in a shelter. It's easy for people not to mind. She isn't very likable.

I know a hundred women who make Job look like a crybaby.

Love,
Jean

September 3, 1989

Dear Shana,

I think if I have lost anything in here it is my sense of time. But then maybe that's all a matter of age and I would have lost it outside as well. Time in its normal passing hardly exists for me anymore. I rarely remember what day it is. Even seasons go by sometimes almost unnoticed, though spring and fall are much too insistent to ignore.

Lance Morrow wrote in a *Time* essay, "Armed with the right of recusal the individual achieves Emersonian self-reliance. He becomes something like a Third World country that has a nuclear capability; he can commit the annihilation of his choice in the privacy of his own mind." I find the thought of myself as a Third World country in here eminently fitting. Though my letters to you often don't sound like it, I do annihilate "in the privacy of my own mind" much of the ugliness and loneliness, and in its place are moments and hours of peace, new ideas, and new concerns. And always there are flashes of yesterday, a smell, a taste, a nothing at all, and suddenly I am transported to a moment with my dollhouse or a walk on the beach or the squirrels in a large oak tree right outside my window at college and so many moments with Hy. For a long time they didn't come back; now they come whether I will it or not. I don't consciously try to bring them back. I don't moon about yesterday; they are simply part of today.

I was always aware in some strange way that the complete peaceful happiness of moments with Hy couldn't last. I don't know how I knew. Wisdom has never been one of my strong points. Endurance is my forte, but I always knew. There was always sadness affixed to the other side of happiness. And I never took an instant for granted. I was always wonderfully aware of happiness and grateful. Perhaps that's why the moments of it come back so perfectly preserved.

"Armed with the right of recusal," the time in here has not gone by nearly as slowly as I supposed it would. I think of time today not in terms of how much of it is lost but how little is left.

Perhaps that's why I've just rewritten my will. It suddenly seemed very important. Joel Aurnou* has the one I wrote before I came here. Though I wrote him years ago and asked him to return it and other personal letters of mine he holds, he refuses to. The will he holds has little bearing on my life today, but I want all the papers back. It looks as though I'll have to sue for them. I'm afraid he clings to them in the hope that after my death he can sell them to a collector of trivia. Prison doesn't have a monopoly on unpleasantness.

Love,
Jean

*The lawyer who represented Jean Harris at her trial.

September 10, 1989

Dear Shana,

I read a wonderful essay today written by Philip Dunne for *Harvard* magazine entitled "The Effects of Superstrings on Victorian Morality." Mr. Dunne is in his eighties and doesn't suppose old age confers wisdom. "Nevertheless," he writes, "throughout history old age has enjoyed and abused the pre-rogative and pleasure of mourning the present as it reveres the past. Cicero was not the first to cry, '*O Tempora, O Mores*,' nor will I by any means be the last. Cataline lives!"

Is it just old age that makes me so fearful of the future I see us blundering into at such a pace—is it too many books and too many newspapers or merely nine years of prison life and prison talk? Whatever it is, I am fearful.

When I see prison women and their many relatives with little education and no marketable skills having their fifth or seventh or tenth baby; when I hear young mothers admit they used drugs all the time they were pregnant; when I read *The Broken Cord* and think of the future of the children of alcohol-ics and when I see the so-called haves with their small families lacking the courage to even suggest that none of us has a God-given right to bear every child we can conceive, I worry. And so should others. Can any thinking person say that family planning is a form of genocide and/or racism?

Love,
Jean

September 22, 1989

Dear Shana,

Here we go again. Another memo "to avoid further confu-sion" about what can and can't be worn in the Visiting Room. It's the third one this year, I believe, though everyone seemed to know what could be worn until they started all this ex-plaining.

This memo gives Webster's definition of a shirt—"a gar-ment for the upper body having a collar, sleeves, front opening and tails long enough to be tucked in"—and defines a blouse as "a loose-fitting shirt which may button in the back or have no collar and a squared bottom not meant to be tucked in." The state shirt or white personal shirts or blouses will be permitted in the Visiting Room. No shoulder pads, lining, stuffing, or rhinestone decorations or neck opening that drape on the shoulders.

"Further, no headbands will be permitted. Barrettes are allowed." No T-shirts, jerseys, rugbys, tank tops, or "tops of this nature" are permitted. "T-shirts, etc., may be worn under the required shirt for warmth, but the T-shirt or blouse may not be removed or opened beyond the second button. A back-opening blouse is to be closed completely." No feelin' around in this women's prison!

"Leg warmers and thermal underwear are not permitted in the Visiting Room." Also permitted now: "A white or green button-down sweater." God help us, what is a button-down sweater? I have button-down shirts that open all the way down the front and some with only three buttons at the neck. The Superintendent says a sweater that buttons at the neck or shoulder is acceptable. The CO who opens the door says, "It ain't." It's hard enough to decide what is truth. What the hell is a "button-down" sweater is one ambiguity too many.

Love,
Confused

October 3, 1989

Dear Shana,

I felt rotten last night and had them lock me in at eight-fifteen so I could go right to bed. I was lucky and went right to sleep. At midnight I was awakened with a start by someone banging on my metal door, then opening it. It was a CO announcing, "I got a lock here for you. You gotta sign for it." "A what?" "A lock for your lockbox. Everybody's got to have one." "I already have a lock. In fact, I have two, and I never use them." "You gotta take it, and you gotta sign for it—four different places." "I don't want it, and I won't use it." "Doesn't matter. You gotta take it." I got up, signed in all four places, took the lock, and climbed back into bed. The CO had my door locked again and went on down the corridor, waking fifty-nine other women in the process. It was ten after twelve.

We haven't enough soap, we haven't any cleanser, we don't have any rags to clean with, but by God, we all have locks. Locks that, incidentally, would make better weapons than some of the things we aren't allowed to have. It was after one o'clock when he finished our floor, and he still had other floors to go to. He did finally call the Watch Commander to see if he should go on waking everyone up. The lieutenant on duty said, "Go ahead and wake 'em." The locks could easily have been given out at the 6:00 A.M. count, the 12:30 P.M. count, the 5:30 P.M. count, or the 10:00 P.M. count. But the lieutenant felt the middle of the night was somehow more appropriate. It was close to three when everyone finally had been given a lock, in many cases something they neither needed nor wanted.

Love,
Jean

October 8, 1989

Dear Shana,

They raided the Parenting Center last night. Among other things, they have taken our sewing machine because it suddenly occurred to some genius that we could make a dress with a sewing machine and then we could slip out the front door disguised as a visitor. One can only hope none of them is thinking too hard when they see an old rerun of *Gone with the Wind*. They'll take all the curtains away and then the bedspreads and then the sheets and then and then. No one has explained to them that you can make a dress with needle and thread, too. Maybe the needles go next.

I'm afraid their own ineptitude gives rise to much of their paranoia. They've also announced that they are going to start counting the number of balls of yarn we have. I think thirty, or twenty, is to be the limit. Consequently, every knitter is presently sitting in the Rec Room rewinding yarn to make five balls look like one. They haven't announced yet how many ounces each ball must weigh, so at the moment one ball of yarn may contain ten normal balls and still satisfy the memo requirements. Family and friends may no longer send yarn, neither some they had at home nor some they bought at the store. Yarn must come from the manufacturer or be sent by the yarn store. In the past eight years, old and new friends have sent hundreds of pounds of yarn to me for women all over the facility. No more. In the vain effort to keep out drugs once again, the indigent women are punished.

What little fabric was once permitted in is also contraband now. You can't sew, and you're limited as to knitting. The raid was especially annoying to me because I had just made a pair of kitchen curtains for the cabin and they were seized along with our sewing machine. It was plain that those two little pieces of material were kitchen curtains, but they are now locked safely away with all the other prison contraband. One trembles to think what danger they might have caused society.

In the meantime, Liz Claiborne donated five industrial sewing machines, thinking, as any normal person would, that women in prison are permitted to sew. I'm told those machines have now gone to one of the men's prisons. That's where our clothes are made. Apparently it hasn't yet occurred to anyone in high places that men, too, can sew a dress and escape in it disguised as a woman.

The tragedy is that after all this foolishness comes to pass, the prison drug trade goes on and on. It's usually just the people trying to make an honest dollar or get to their job or play it straight who are pounded on. It's so easy to hurt the people who are trying to do better and so easy for the others to go right on ignoring the rules.

Love,
Jean

October 12, 1989

Dear Shana,

When we first started planning the Intensive Parenting course, I thought it was very farsighted and wise of us to acknowledge that the first part of the course should be devoted to the mothers' self-esteem. We were pioneers, or so I thought. With a little reading, we soon discovered thousands of schools were "teaching" self-esteem, too. There are self-esteem notebooks for all ages, and self-esteem games and self-esteem videos, the works. America is "doing" self-esteem. Some people have begun to observe that we've gone too far.

I guess it was a combination of conviction and my nose being out of joint that prompted me to scribble in my notes today, "As self-esteem becomes the whole subject, it is harder and harder to teach anything of substance." Obviously the class finds it more interesting to reminisce and consider their own lives than to hear about the needs of their children. I realize the two are not mutually exclusive. Perhaps the class is learning more about parenting by considering some of the holes in their own lives.

In my book the one legitimate way to develop self-esteem is to do something you can be proud of. Being recognized and appreciated, not constantly put down, is important, too, but the fruit of your own honest labor is what self-esteem springs from. Perhaps I'm writing this because my feelings are hurt and I want you to tell me I'm a good girl—as my mother used to do. I received a letter from a stranger today who had just read my books and wants me to know I am far too critical of the women here and that I expect too much of them. "After all, you were a role model and look where you are today. You expect too much of everyone, yourself included. You have to start with the women where they are."

Not expecting enough of people is the greatest put-down of all. Many of the women here had no childhood. "I been on the streets all my life." How many times have I heard that? Now they have children of their own, as few as one, as many as fourteen, among my particular students. Their children need a mother. They haven't time for her to go back and go through the whole growing-up process. There have to be some leaps of faith. I think they are capable of learning anything I expect of them. But it's oh so hard to get them to want to learn or to believe in their own capability as firmly as I do. The lack of will to learn has hardened around some of them like those new plastic toothpaste containers. You can see the person inside, but you can't touch it.

I wish I were physically stronger than I am. I find myself

backing down, folding my tent, and quietly slipping away from the classroom. Scratch that. I'm not going to fold my tent. Not yet, anyway.

Love,
Grimly Determined

October 28, 1989

Dear Shana,

You're right. I can't just expect a lot from students. I have to start by figuring out where the students are. You tell me where they are. Here are some of the women in our Intensive Parenting class.

Bertha is a pretty woman, though AIDS is giving her a progressively gaunt look. She has naturally light blond hair and a clear complexion and a ready smile, though she has less to smile about than anyone in the class, and that's going some. Her grandmother, mother, sister, and she have all served time at Bedford prison. Her fourteen-year-old daughter has just had a baby. I had known little about her early life until we began talking about family life in the Intensive Parenting class. Lucia asked the women about family customs they remembered with pleasure, things the family did year after year. Bertha said, "There wasn't any kinda customs in my family. Every day was different, every day was different people around, we didn't do nothing on birthdays or Christmas." She stopped for a minute, then added, "I wouldn't even tell you what it was like in my family." She told us, "My daughter ask me one day, 'Ma, what's a normal family like,' and I told her, 'I don't know. Honey, I don't know. I don't know's I ever seen one.'"

Jennifer is the WASP in the group, white, college educated,

outsmarted herself on a computer and ended up in here. Still on the subject of families, Lucia asked them about family values, what their parents taught them to value most. Was getting a good education as important as "keeping up with the Joneses?" There were some embarrassed smiles at that question. Obviously they knew what the term meant. Some agreed people naturally like to have the same stuff the people around them have or maybe the people on television try to get you to buy. Jennifer said, "Keeping up with the Joneses was not a problem in my house. My father told us we are the Joneses."

Linda is here for writing bad checks. "I never kept the money," she insists. "I gave it to my mother and father. They were in on it. I did it for them. They knew what I was doing." Oddly enough, she says she feels no anger toward them. In fact, she mentioned on several occasions that "my father is my role model. I want to be just like him. He does his thing; he don't bother about others. I wanna be like that."

Georgette broadened the scope of rituals and customs from childhood to say how she hated what seems to have become a custom at her son's school, where there's always a big "rumble" after basketball games. Her son was in one last week, when the other team, the losers, brought out knives and threatened to use them. Tiny, who is not only tiny but young and usually very quiet, said, "That's not so bad. You always have rumbles with your big rival. At our school we used to put dead cats in their lockers and set their stuff on fire. That don't mean anything."

Fatima sits with her head on her desk and her arms wrapped around her head. She spends most of her time in the position you might assume in an air raid. Sometimes she's asleep; sometimes she's awake. She is the walking wounded. She has been used, jeered at, beaten, ignored, you name it. Whatever the abuse, it's part of her childhood memory. And it hasn't stopped. Three inmates recently dragged her from her cell into one of theirs and tried to sodomize her. She speaks haltingly and so quietly one can hardly hear her. You always have to ask her to repeat. There isn't enough love in all the world to make her whole again. She will always be the walking wounded. She has three children.

Jerry simply smiles or laughs when you ask her how she was disciplined as a child. "What discipline?" she asks. "Wasn't nobody around to pay us no mind. Wasn't nobody cared what we did." She is also one who sleeps during class. As an infant, she was given away to an aunt by her mother, and went back to her mother at age seven, when the aunt died. As one more mouth to feed, she was disliked, resented, and rejected by everyone in the family. At the age of twelve she was labeled "incorrigible" and sent away to a youth home. By then she was deep into drugs. "I never come up for air. I was on it all the time." She has three children. She was on drugs all the time she carried them. She's twenty-two.

Glenda was one of sixteen children. She has three kids of her own now. She had them by the time she was eighteen. She admits she used crack every day she was pregnant. "I knew it was wrong. I hated myself for doing it, but I couldn't leave it alone." Three other women admit the same thing but say, like Glenda, that their kids are "just fine." "They always tryin' to put a guilt trip on me, sayin' everything my daughter does wrong is because I took drugs. But she's okay—she's all right. Nothin' wrong with my kids."

Virgie talks about how she and her brother were always left alone at night, and scared. "My brother kept a loaded gun behind his bed from the time he was six. Nighttime, when we'd hear somethin' on the steps or a knockin' at the door, he'd get the gun and get me, and we'd wait in the corner and see what's gonna happen."

I am a stranger in a strange land, Shana, and yet I am part of it, too. I guess we're all strangers in a strange land. We spend a lifetime adjusting or refusing to adjust—growing or not growing, I'm not sure which I am doing in here. I think I'm just waiting—waiting to return to my own land. Hoping I live long enough to see it again, if it still exists.

Love,
Jean

November 1, 1989

Dear Shana,

After years of eating alone, dinnertime has become a pleasant and civil time for me, thanks to Sheila, Maria, and Jan. We eat together in the Recreation Room, pooling our edible resources from home. Fruit and vegetables are what we miss most, so they make up the large percentage of the thirty-five pounds a month each of us is permitted to receive.

I do almost no cooking, but I'm a competent cleaner-upper. I think my cooking is limited by a combination of the generally accepted theory that I'm so absentminded I may burn the place down, and a little leftover mythology that followed me here about my lifetime of money and servants, which caused me to have little contact with a kitchen. Whatever the reason, I am treated like the village idiot when I enter the kitchen. It used to make me cross. Now I just figure, what the hell. I have discovered what many children learn early on; if nothing is expected of you, so much the better. You don't have to do anything.

Some of the women, including Maria and Jan, can make very good corn bread and biscuits on top of the stove. Dinner is our one meal of the day. Like so many women, we don't go to the prison dining room. Breakfast and lunch are a nibble on whatever we have. You have only to look at me to know I don't go hungry. Many of the women on the floor do as we do, so in spite of the crowding in the kitchen dinner is decent and almost normal. We look forward to it.

Love,
Jean

November 5, 1989

Dear Shana,

When we talk about the possibility of legalizing drugs, the young girls who are here because of crack, and will tell you very openly they can't wait to go out and get more, think it's a great idea. For the most part, the women who are mothers are overwhelmingly against it, whether drugs brought them in here or not. Fear hasn't kept them away from drugs, but fear makes them want to keep their children away from it. Many of them agree sadly with Jennie, who said, "Far's I'm concerned, it's legal already. It's everywhere my kids goes, at school, in the school yard, in the halls where they live, the grocery store, everywhere. It couldn't be more available if it was legal."

Certainly taking the great quantities of money out of it would help, though ultimately someone would still be selling it. Obviously prohibition doesn't work, and the fallout from it this time is worse than it was in the twenties and thirties. The billions of dollars spent trying to enforce laws we know we can't enforce are lost to social programs we badly need. And for reasons that have to do with single parenthood and other female problems, women are coming to prison with drug charges three times faster than men.

America has been hooked for two hundred years on a dream of moral purity in normal human beings we must know by now they will never deliver, and I mean people of all races, creeds, socioeconomic groups, and previous conditions of servitude. The result is we win the hypocrisy sweepstakes while our crime rates and prison rates soar above those in every other country in the world we consider "Western" and "civilized."

By legalizing some of the things we now criminalize, I think we would take back some of the control of our streets that we've lost. Did you know that in Holland, where prostitution is legal, less than 1 percent of prostitutes test positive for the AIDS virus? In New York City, between 30 and 40 percent test positive.

It isn't easy to say something you've thought was "wrong" all your life, "wrong" in the sense that your grandmother used that word, should be made legal. But legal doesn't necessarily mean right. It means permitted by law, as the law recognizes the needs and foibles of society. I think both drugs and prostitution should be legalized, though I must confess that an annoying small voice still occasionally says, "But on the other hand . . ." Bigots have the best of it, Shana—no question about it.

Love,
Jean

November 10, 1989

Dear Shana,

In spite of all our new learning, the nature versus nurture argument seems to be as unresolved today as it was when I first took an interest in it forty years ago, and long before that as well. I never bought Father Flanagan's motto "There's no such thing as a bad boy," but I'd hate to believe there's such a thing as a bad infant. That borders on science fiction.

I read Stanton Samenow's book *Inside the Criminal Mind* not long ago and more recently his article "Before It's Too Late," and I find them very disturbing. He writes:

> Crime resides within the minds of human beings and is not caused by social conditions. . . . My central premise is that children become anti-social by choice. Lying, fighting, stealing and other forms of destructive behavior are willful acts. . . . The toddler chooses whether or not to obey parental orders forbidding him to touch valuable household possessions. . . . As time passes the choices become more numerous and complex. Parents are often faulted for causing a child's irresponsible behavior, when it is the child himself who made the choice. . . . Defiance, excitement seeking can begin in pre-schoolers and by the time a child is eight he knows right from wrong and chooses one way or the other. . . . The environment from which a person comes is less crucial than the choice the individual makes as he responds to the environment. . . . Aggression at age 8 is the best predictor of aggression at age 19 irrespective of IQ, social class or parents.

Prison statistics don't corroborate the last part. If true, it tells us, at best, that the justice system is not evenhanded, and, at worst, that poor people have dumb, dishonest kids and the rich and middle class have bright, honest kids. And that's nonsense.

The babies born into our prison nursery, assuming they are the lucky ones whose mothers received prenatal care and didn't drink or use drugs while they were pregnant, are just as bright and educable as those born in Scarsdale or East Seventy-second Street. I watch many of them for a year and see them climb all the intellectual stairs of a good, healthy, normal baby if mother is doing her job of nurturing.

Of course, there's a point at which the child moves into drive and parents are no longer responsible for her actions, but who's to say where the point is. I'm sure it differs with each of us. I think the human brain will always be the ultimate mystery, but one thing I have learned in here beyond a shadow of a doubt: The heart is the true center of man; compassion is the beginning of humanity—without it all that toolmaking is a monumental waste of time.

Fondly,
Jean

November 12, 1989

Dear Shana,

A young man named Francis Fukuyama, a State Department policy planner, has written a much-discussed article suggesting that Western, liberal, capitalist democracy is what the world yearns for; communism in Eastern Europe is on the way out, and we are therefore approaching what may be "the end of history." I haven't read the whole thing yet, but what I have read I find thought-provoking. Its basic premise is that the world wants to become like us and once we're all like us the world will be a pretty boring place, no fresh new ideas, no struggle of new ideologies, only "economic calculation, the endless solving of technical problems, environmental concerns and the satisfaction of sophisticated consumer demands . . . neither art nor philosophy, just the perpetual caretaking of the museum of human history."

Unfortunately, America's ego being what it is, there may be many among us complacent enough to agree. In my opinion, the world may want to have what we have, but I doubt it wants to be like us. America isn't the commodious playpen it was even a generation ago, and the reputation abroad of our national social values is not an enviable one.

Some people suggested that the French Revolution would be the end of history. A lot of people claimed communism would be the end of history. George Orwell, describing his fictional Oceania in his novel *1984*, wrote, "History has stopped. Nothing exists except an endless present, in which the party is always right." Today, what keeps East Berliners pouring into West Germany is all that nifty stuff in the store windows, not a nation "yearning to breathe free." Somewhere along the time line we've begun to think of capitalism and democracy as the same thing, and that's a large error.

Mr. Fukuyama's picture of our future seems to me to be a mirror image of Marx's predictions. Like Hegel, they both believe in a great historical scheme that will one day win the world, but Marx believed that dialectical materialism would lead inexorably to the demise of capitalism and the rise of communism. One suggested the rich would roll over and play dead. The other suggests that the poor will roll over and play dead. I don't think either one will.

Fukuyama's article has aroused my latent interest in economics, stemming first from four years of reading economics at college and then from fairly widespread travel and observations abroad, including a book I wrote about Russia thirty years ago. I find myself combing books and papers for information on Eastern Europe's struggle toward an open-market economy as well as the state of our own economy. It's strangely stimulating and somehow has become quite important to me. To each his own.

Love
Jean

November 22, 1989

Dear Shana,

I've been reading the parts of Robert Caro's book *Means of Ascent* that ran in *The New Yorker*. It documents Lyndon Johnson's driving ambition for power and his first giant step in that direction when he won a Texas Senate seat by manipulating voters and votes. Actually that's a euphemism. If Caro's facts are correct, and they certainly seem to be, Johnson lied, cheated, and stole to climb the ladder that led him to the presidency. Does anyone who makes the wheels turn play fair? Is it childish to suppose they could? Is old age the age of disillusionment because then you haven't the strength to react to life as you might have at thirty? Or am I now a rare, fossilized specimen who grew up believing that people were good and the system worked, and never pondered about why Justice is always blindfolded?

I think how Johnson's two daughters must feel about the book. They may not read it, but they won't be able to avoid at least hearing about it. Will they be ashamed, or will they only ache for him? We all have something or someone to ache for. Don't we?

Jean

November 29, 1989

Dear Shana,

It had never occurred to me to question the purpose of a prison library. I naturally assumed it was to encourage people to read and to make books available to them so that they could read. Donna sent me some articles that appeared this month in the *Library Journal* and the *Wilson Library*

Journal, both publications I would never see without her kindness.

The correctional library consultant in the Colorado State Library, William Coyle, has written a book on prison libraries in which he recommends that we erase "the shopworn assumption that public libraries should be the model of choice for prison libraries, or that inmate needs and preferences should be the chief consideration." This ridiculous liberal thinking, he notes, is from the crazy sixties and has reduced prison libraries to mere recreation centers where inmates trade westerns and gothic novels. To the argument that prison reading should provide enjoyment and release, Mr. Coyle's considered judgment is brief. He writes, "Bullshit." He writes with so little respect for prisoners one would think he was running for Congress. His utter contempt for people in prison is unquestionably a great vote getter and just as unquestionably a way to perpetuate the crippling self-hate that helps to bring prisoners back to prison again and again and again. One critique of Coyle's book is headlined "Throw the Book at 'Em." A splendid way to attack illiteracy.

What Coyle is saying essentially is that a prison library cannot be recreational and educational, too. What nonsense. Any good library is both. The library here at Bedford, which is a good library, is both. Thanks to Rosa, there is a good basic reference collection for both college and high school students, an excellent clipping file, microfiche, lending facilities with local libraries, discussion groups of books and current affairs, self-directed work, good current films, an AIDS self-help group, as well as ample recreational reading. Rosa is always there to open new doors for the women and to treat their individual interests with respect. Unfortunately, I have reason to believe our library is not a typical prison library.

Mr. Coyle seems to want to return to a version of thought control and to pick out prisoners' reading for them. In the first American prisons and until well into this century the Bible and other religious literature and temperance tracts made up the large majority of the books prisoners could have. The purpose of reading was right thinking and moral reform, and the prison chaplain usually served as the librarian.

In 1938 a German named Hans Lowe wrote a book entitled *The Purposes of a Prison Library* in which he recommended, as Coyle does, that a prison library should instruct the prisoners in the goals of the state. On his list of most recommended was Hitler's *Mein Kampf* and *The Life of Hermann Göring*. He did allow one novel every two weeks. Coyle would remove all novels. "Their families can send them paperbacks." There is often a "let 'em eat cake" attitude in writing about what's best for prisoners. I hope not too many decision-making people within the correctional system take Mr. Coyle's book with more than the grain of salt that it's worth.

Love,
Jean

December 3, 1989

Dear Shana,

Virginia has made many lovely wreaths using wild potato vines that grow on the hill, pressed flowers retrieved from the garbage, bits of ribbon, whatever. They are meant to be gifts, but today, when she tried to mail them out, the Package Room CO told her, "Per the captain the wild potato vine is state property and inmates can't send state property out of the facility."

You can't make up garbage like that. You have to hear it, as the ladies say, "fresh outta yo' mouth." The captain is the same one who saw me eating mulberries one summer day from a large, fruitful mulberry tree and came running up to me. "Here! Stop that! You can't eat those." "But it's laden with them, and if we don't eat them, they'll go to waste." "They're supposed to go to waste," she snapped.

What kind of rocks do you turn over to discover minds like that?

Puzzled,
Jean

December 10, 1989

Dear Shana,

Two weeks ago I fell down going to work and tore a hole in the knee of my brand-new state pants. If I were home and they were my own pants, I would take a small piece of fabric out of the underside of the pant-leg hem and patch it. No problem. But nothing that simple is acceptable here. For the past few months the cause célèbre in here has had to do with women altering their state clothes. Some do and always will shorten and tighten the skirts. With high-heeled shoes and lacy little socks or fancy hose, they look for all the world as they did on their favorite street corner. And they mince and wiggle past the COs as only they can. Slacks they make narrow to the point you'd swear the wearer was sewn in after putting them on. The foot couldn't possibly have made it through such a narrow opening. The sewing is rough at best, rarely with matching thread. Making the garment tight is the whole point. Sewing a fine seam is not.

The rules say you cannot alter state clothes. But to stop and write a Charge Sheet for every woman whose fanny is encased like a green sausage in pants or skirt, ready to split open with the next deep breath, would disrupt the normal flow of prison activity. Hence, they are rarely written. A special day, not announced in advance, was set aside a few weeks ago to handle the problem once and for all.

There were no classes held. Everyone was locked in until COs arrived on your floor; then the inmates went into the Rec Room, and the cells were minutely searched for clothes that had been altered. These were seized as contraband. Later, inmates were called down individually, made to claim their clothes, rip out all alterations, and receive a Charge Sheet. Some were also made to pay for clothes that had been cut. Within a week after this big police action, there were just as many tight skirts as there had been before the search. But a good deal of time had been wasted, which always makes people feel something of merit has happened.

Since I like loose, even baggy clothes, I never alter state clothes except to put in a hem. Now, what to do with my new state pants? If I went ahead on my own and sewed on a small patch, the "Witch of Endor," a CO who strip-searches us when we leave the Visiting Room, would undoubtedly see it and give me another Charge Sheet.

Instead, I wrote to the State Shop seeking guidance and counseling. A week or so later I was called to the store. I explained my predicament, told them what I would do if they were my own pants. Without a moment's hesitation, the staff person in charge took the torn pants, deposited them in the wastebasket, and gave me a new pair.

Love,
Embittered Taxpayer

December 26, 1989

Dear Shana,

I was sent back to my cell today to change my shirt because CO Endor said, "Shirts can't have a turtleneck." I don't happen to possess a shirt with a turtleneck, though there isn't any rule that says you can't wear one. The blouse I was wearing is my favorite one because it's good-looking and David gave it to me for Christmas three years ago. I have probably worn it twenty times since the July memo on what blouses we can wear into the Visiting Room. I wore it yesterday, Christmas. Furthermore, I had checked it out with the deputy superintendent, who found it "just fine." No one had ever questioned that it was permissible on all counts. Now suddenly its cowl neckline was called a turtleneck, and I couldn't see my visitor until I walked back up the hill to my cell to change it. I was too angry to sit and visit. For the first time in nine years I told them to send my visitor away.

Sergeant Connely was standing nearby, and I turned to him for help. He mumbled that it looked like a cowl neckline to him, but for such a weighty decision he needed a third opinion, so he called another sergeant, explained what had happened, that the blouse "looks like a cowl neckline to me," said, "Yes, sir, yes, sir," a few times, hung up, and said, "He says go up and change the blouse." Only in prison do people determine the appearance of something they have never seen. I was sent back to my cell like an errant child, and the Witch of Endor smiled and gloated, knowing she had lied and gotten away with it. Three COs and two sergeants actually played an active or passive role in that performance, and not one of the five had the decency to try to stop it or showed any concern for truth.

The next day, I went again to a visit, this time wearing a state blouse to save further angst. The witch was on duty again and now knew, as everyone else involved knew, that she had deliberately lied to harass me. I didn't speak to her. She walked up to me and said, "Well, it's off-white, anyway, so you can't wear it."

At a certain point, employees like this can cause administration more trouble than the inmates do. And it's virtually impossible to fire them.

How unkind it all is—and so totally counterproductive to the competent administration of any kind of an institution. It's a weary end to a weary year.

Love,
Jean

January 5, 1990

Dear Shana,

Lucia, who does all the coordinating and most of the teaching in our Intensive Parenting course, sent all the members of the class and all of us who do some of the teaching a Christmas card. Today a memo came from the Superintendent saying that her permit to teach will be renewed *this time, but in the future* she must remember that staff may *not* give anything—letter, card, or gift of any description—to any inmates.

Incoming mail is all opened, ostensibly to check for contraband, especially money and stamps. Apparently the mail room also takes time to check out and report something as innocent as a Christmas card from a teacher who works ten hours a week for three-month stretches with her students and gets to know them far better than their counselors ever could. What hypocrisy, and what a waste of time, trying to mandate unkindness. There's quite enough here without requiring it.

Love,
Jean

January 10, 1990

Dear Shana,

As it was bound to be, the dress code has been changed again, the third time in less than nine months. Now we may go back to wearing colored shirts, blouses, and sweaters in the Visiting Room, with the usual caveat that they not be blue, gray, black, or orange, the colors of guard uniforms—their raincoats are orange. So much time and paper and money are spent, only to keep us on edge and to harass us. There is the terrible and constant fear in here that we are not being punished enough, that permitting us the luxury of looking like women is a sign of weakness in them that may make the public angry and loosen their grip on their jobs. If the same dogged determination were spent teaching us to read and write and get to work on time, we might over time make it possible to build new schools instead of more prisons, but that, my friend, is most certainly not the goal of the prison system.

Jean

January 12, 1990

Dear Shana,

Claude Brown, who wrote *Manchild in the Promised Land*, wrote recently in the *Los Angeles Times*, "The average prison inmate cannot afford to stay out of prison." I don't buy that, but I do think it's reasonable to say that many prison inmates don't know how to make an honest living. The reason for that starts with the qualities of character and ability one is born with. Bad parents and bad neighborhoods play a big part. Granted, most of them have had many more strikes against them than you or I, or people like us, and climbing out of the holes their lives have fallen into is a hard climb. Prisons should be the places where inmates are required to do the things they haven't done on their own. Here you can mop floors for fifteen years or sling hash or deliver the mail if you choose to. Many people leave prison still unable to read or write. Many Hispanics, some of whom may have lived in this country for ten or fifteen years, leave still unable to speak, read, or write English. People who have never earned an honest dollar leave still having no marketable skill. In many cases this is because there was no access to skill-building classes. In other cases it was because they were not required to respond to the opportunities offered.

If you ask 100 prisoners what their most important goal is, the vast majority will tell you, "To get out!" This being so, there's no better motivation for the rest of their lives than to be told they cannot win parole until they have a *legal*, marketable skill. (Ethel is quite complacent about her ability to "cut" cocaine. "That straight-up cocaine gonna kill you. You gotta cut it just right. There's a lotta people out there won't buy any cocaine 'cept I cut it.") Hence, the word "legal" is important.

It would give them goals and hope, two things New York State prisoners especially lack since New York State has no merit-time program. In other states, prisoners can earn time off their minimum sentence by fulfilling stated constructive tasks. Merit Time, in other words, is earned, as the name implies. In New York State, what is called Merit Time is automatically given by cutting time off the back of the maximum sentence. We don't earn it, but we can lose it. Since many prisoners have life as their maximum, one to life, five to life, fifteen to life, whatever, for them there is no such thing as Merit Time. In short, New York State provides no motivation whatsoever for prisoners to use prison time wisely and well.

You can be valedictorian of your Mercy College graduating class, the local college that offers courses there through a B.A. or B.S. Two out of the past three years a Bedford woman has graduated with a 4.0 grade point average. You can tutor many women, give aid and comfort to the dying, serve women in the law library, do every conceivable useful thing you can think of, and a woman who sleeps around, yells obscenities at the COs, steals from the prison kitchen, steals from the commissary, steals from neighbors, bats her lovers around viciously, can be first out on parole. Some women go out on parole directly from lock, where they are supposedly being punished for any of the above. There is little question that many will return.

Prisons work the way companies do that build obsolescence into their products so you have to buy them again and again. In prison the obsolescence period is from one to three years. Recidivism is usually determined by how many return within that time frame. I know of women who have been rearrested, with a new felony charge, within twenty-four hours of being paroled. In time, customers resent and react to planned obsolescence where needed products are concerned. But all the commonsense rules of the marketplace are ignored where prisons are concerned. Apparently we really don't care that they don't work, are often counterproductive, and deplete the public treasury to the detriment of social programs we urgently need.

According to the National Institute of Justice, the recidivism rate in state prisons is now just over 66 percent, that is, people who return to prison within three years with a new felony conviction.

One is tempted to wonder whether their return is not simply part of the prearranged system. If I didn't know how abysmal their talent for long-range planning is, I would be sure of it. The legitimate uses of authority are too often wasted, used to bully instead of to train, to make better, to develop self-discipline, in short, to do what they advertise, correct.

Love,
Jean

January 20, 1990

Dear Shana,

I walked up the hill with a woman called Sherry this noon. She looked sadder than usual, though her face often wears the look of a woman who has known very little joy in her life. "They had to cancel the trailer visit with my mother and kids. I can't put any more on her than she's already got. My sister's smoked out and on the critical list in the hospital. So now my mother's got her three kids as well as my four to look after, and one of my brother's, too. Eight kids she's raisin' and she already raised fifteen of her own. I can't ask her to come up here, too. There's nothin' I can do for my sister 'cept write her a letter—maybe she'd read it, maybe she wouldn't."

I had never heard the expression "smoked out" before, but Sherry added, "It's the crack. She probably won't ever give it up. It's too much on my mother, and there's nothin' I can do. Nothin' I can do."

Precious announced yesterday, "I'm not gonna be a social worker! Never! I can't stand one more sad story or one more of these women comin' down and askin' me to find their kids, get 'em here for a visit. That last bitch in here been on the street using crack and hasn't seen her children in three years, three years! Now she's in prison and off the crack a little while and now she tells you how much she loves 'em. If I told them the truth, they'd punch me in the mouth. The truth is their kids are better off without them. . . . Well, I don't know. . . . Your mother is your mother. Maybe the foster home they end up in isn't any better. I can't think about these kids anymore. It breaks your heart. I thought sure I was gonna do social work once I get outta here, but no more. I've heard enough. No way!"

She means it at the moment, but not for long. I think Precious does some of the most valuable counseling that goes on in here concerning foster care. Her desk is near mine, and

I hear her talk to troubled women day after day with a kind of wisdom and honesty one could wish there were more of in here.

Love,
Jean

January 25, 1990

Dear Shana,

Mr. Fukuyama has written a short (eight-page) response to his many critics and admirers. People took him seriously for the most part, even if they didn't agree with him. He explains that his conviction about history ending with the "victory of democratic egalitarianism" over all other political and economic philosophies is based on a "concept of altered human nature." Why the word "egalitarianism" doesn't make the White House and the State Department edgy, I don't know. He doesn't define it, and he doesn't explain why the most recent and most popular president in our history was less burdened by "democratic egalitarian consciousness" than any American president in our history. He also doesn't explain how we are going to spread this lovely egalitarianism around, even to the children Jonathan Kozol describes as "born to the implacable inheritance of a diminished destiny," children whom we are now producing in large numbers.

It is fascinating to me how Fukuyama has borrowed from Marx. The concept of altered human nature is right out of *Das Kapital*. Anyone who has taken a quick trip through Moscow has heard the party line about "the new Soviet Man" who, with his altered human nature, will live happily under a system of "from each according to his ability to each according to his needs." It didn't work, or human nature didn't change quite enough, and it's the main reason communism fell on its face. He also doesn't answer why, if it's our philosophy and not our store windows that are sweeping the world, it is that only 50 percent of our citizens bother to vote for the president, about 35 percent for senators, 30 percent for congressmen, and sometimes as few as 15–20 percent for local officers.

He hasn't suggested how well "democratic egalitarianism" will sit with us when there are 15 billion humans on earth instead of 5 billion. I wonder how all the "democratic egalitarianists" will be programmed to feel about birth control then. Survival of the fittest is an idea whose time could really come. I personally can't see anything approaching boredom for the foreseeable, even the geologic, future.

Fukuyama's writing has really wound me up. Jim calls it my neurosis. I've started a "Fukuyama File," and it's growing fat.

It's too bad Tom Wolfe has already used the title *Bonfire of the Vanities*. It would make a splendid and fitting title for the final, definitive history of the United States. There's still time to change that, but only if we look to our children.

Love,
Jean

January 29, 1990

Dear Shana,

An article in the *Wall Street Journal* today about the frightening increase of women coming to prison for violent crimes is headlined "You've Come a Long Way, Moll." You just can't beat cute journalism. But then not many of us molls read the *Wall Street Journal*, so it isn't very important.

Fondly,
Jean

February 10, 1990

Dear Shana,

The Supreme Court handed down a decision a couple of days ago that has a direct bearing on the women I play bingo with. The court determined that a prison physician can now force a mental patient to take mind-altering drugs. I would like to see the doctor who could make Georgine or Pat or Evelyn take anything they didn't want. It would take five strong men, and then they still wouldn't swallow it. I've heard them say many times, "I ain't takin' that shit. It make me do this rockin' all night long. . . ." "It make my tongue hang out. . . ." "It don't do no good, anyway. . . . It make me worse. . . ." And since up to now the accepted wisdom has been that you cannot make the women take medicine they refuse, there hasn't been a problem. Now we'll see.

Some of the nurses here are very kind to the women, especially those in the mental ward. They used to have special things for them at Christmas, and cookies and juice after their night medication, until one of the very litigious inmates wrote administration and suggested that the nurses were "bribing" inmates to take their medicine. Immediately a memo came out ordering all the nursing staff *never* to give any kind of cookie, candy, or gift of any description, however small, to inmates at any time. It did many women out of the few personal kindnesses they ever experienced in here. Now that the Supreme Court has spoken, if I were unfortunate enough to be running this place, I'd rescind the memo, and fast. A few cookies might save a lot of grief in the years ahead.

Love,
Jean

February 12, 1990

Dear Shana,

We had a visiting teacher for the Intensive Parenting class today who showed us a device often used in therapy classes called "living statues." Using her own family to explain how it is done, she asked one woman to come up and be her mother. . "You stand there." Another came up to be her father. "And you stand over there." A brother who was her mother's favorite came and stood beside the mother. The brother she was closest to came and stood beside her. Father's favorite stood by him, and thus the whole family was placed in the relationships to one another that she recalls. "There," she said. "This is a living statue of my family." The loudest in the class, the one who never knew her father, the one who told us she had been labeled "incorrigible" at the age of twelve, jumped up enthusiastically. "I wanna do it next. Me next," she said. "Okay, you're my mother, stand there. You're my older brother, get right next to her. She was crazy about him. He couldn't do anything wasn't wonderful. Okay, you're my sister. You stand there. And you're my younger brother, stand near her. Okay, I'll stand here. Now, all of you turn around and have your back facing me. There. That's a living statue of my family."

That, my friend, is a picture of lonely.

Jean

February 18, 1990

Dear Shana,

My stomach is in knots, I'm bone tired, and my year on the Honor Floor seems to be ending the way it began, with my not jumping up quickly enough for the 6:00 A.M. count. I awoke yesterday to a knock on my door. The regular CO who wakes us each morning with a good loud call is off today. I was groggy with sleep and said, "Yes. What do you want?" "Standing count," the voice said. It was dark out. "You don't call standing counts in the middle of the night," I said. We've had some new COs who thought they were to call standing counts every time they walked down the corridor. "Standing count," she repeated. "If you wake up sixty women in the middle of the night," I said, "there'll be chaos up here." As I rolled over to get up, she went on down the hall, taking the standing count. My cell is the first one in the corridor.

I got up, peered at my clock, and finally realized it was 6:00 A.M. I was dressing when the CO, without knocking, pulled back my privacy curtain to warn me she was going to give me a Charge Sheet for not following a direct order. "I called the morning count. That's a direct order." A while later, I was walking toward the Recreation Room. I passed the CO as she was walking into the kitchen. "I can't believe you would threaten a person for not following a direct order when they were obviously not fully awake." "I'm not threatening you," she said. "Of course you are. A Charge Sheet means I could be removed from this floor and sent back to the dormitories. Of course it's a threat." We have been told by administration that a cell is now to be considered a privilege in here. If you lose your cell "for cause," you go back to the dormitory area. "Get outta my face," the CO said, and walked into the kitchen. She didn't take long to write the Charge Sheet. It's one and a half pages long and accuses me of three separate infractions of the rules.

Refusing a direct order 106-10
Interfering with a CO's duties 107-10
Interfering with the taking of the count 112-21

When I went to get my medication today (Tofranil, an antidepressant that I take in addition to Inderal, Cardizem, and Lopid) I was told by the nurse that the combination of those drugs, but especially the Tofranil, can have a sedative effect. "You should have a note on your door to that effect," she said. "Other women do." I assured her I am usually up and reading by 6:00 A.M. Unfortunately, when I'm not, I seem to hit the wrong COs, or rather, they hit me. She volunteered that she would get a letter from the doctor about the effect of the drug I take, and I assured her that I would be grateful.

Love,
Jean

February 22, 1990

Dear Shana,

Connie died of AIDS today. The Christmas gifts she had picked out for her children are still wrapped and sitting in Sister Elaine's office.

Jean

February 23, 1990

Dear Shana,

I have just finished reading Stephen Jay Gould's book *Wonderful Life*. It's a restudy of the Burgess Shale in British Columbia, an ancient limestone deposit dating back to Cambrian time, 530 million years ago. Gould teaches the history of science and paleontology at Harvard, and in studying the many and varied fossils that are found in the Burgess Shale, he digs into the nature of history—no suggestions from him that it's about to end.

His conclusion, along with a great many fascinating draw-ings and data on individual fossils, is that evolution is not a steady progression from tiny to merely interesting to getting bigger and better and ultimately to best (*Homo sapiens*). Evolu-tion is, he concludes, far more a product of chance than many of us may have been taught. If we went back, he writes, and started again with a world of one-celled animals, there probably isn't a chance in millions that we, and the other animals, would turn out the same. Einstein said, "God doesn't play dice with the world," but if Gould is correct, the world, no less wonderful than before, is partly a crapshoot even if God is the one holding the dice. Darwin wrote, "The universe runs by laws with the details, whether good or bad, left to the working out of what we may call chance." One zig instead of a zag 500 million years ago and the whole playing out of life on earth could have been, would have been, completely different.

Gould writes, "We are the offspring of history and must establish our own paths in this most diverse and interesting of conceivable universes—one indifferent to our suffering, and therefore offering us maximal freedom to thrive or fail, in our own chosen way." That pretty well answers the question why bad things happen to good people. It's a humbling image, and a challenging one as well, and a good one for the young to learn early. "You're on your own, Charlie—go for it. But remember, you touch everyone else, and everyone else touches you."

Love,
Jean

February 25, 1990

Dear Shana,

Finally all those courtroom scenes are behind you. You've talked for years about writing the story of your mother's and father's lives, but it always seemed to be set aside while another trial was there to write about. I'm glad those decks are finally cleared, permanently, I hope, and now you can write *Poles Apart*. It's a perfect title for the story. The title usually comes last, doesn't it, sometimes frantically, just before a book goes to press? It's a good omen, I think, to start with just the right title and blessedly, to know no one else is racing to write the same story.

I'll miss our Saturday morning chats if you have to spend a long time in California searching out family history—but I'll look forward to the book.

Fondly,
Jean

February 27, 1990

Dear Shana,

I've been tearing recipes out of magazines for years, not because I'm hungry for the end result but only for the pleasure of imagining myself in a clean kitchen once again and making something for David and Jim.

I save pictures of gardens, too, ones I would so enjoy planting. That collection is growing quite large. I guess it's time to send it to the cabin.

I'll send you some of the pictures of freestanding fireplaces you mentioned you were interested in. There are some very good-looking ones today. I guess we'll eventually need one in the cabin, too. Thinking about a home outside sometimes seems real, and pleasurable. Sometimes it seems like foolish make-believe.

Love,
Jean

March 1, 1990

Dear Shana,

I had my hearing on the charge sheet today before Lieutenant Grant. I was shaking and on the verge of tears before I even went into her office. If she had found me guilty, I would have been removed from the Honor Floor and sent back to one of the dormitories, where there is now double bunking and a large number of young street women here for use and sale of crack. It would be a nightmare!

We went through the usual stuff, testing the recorder to be sure it worked, stating my name and number, the lieutenant announcing that this was a Tier Two hearing for Jean Harris. The Charge Sheet is two pages long and says I am guilty of three separate charges: refusal to obey a direct order, keeping a CO from discharging her duties, and interfering with the taking of the count.

What did I plead? "Not guilty. Not guilty. Not guilty." The irony of this farce eats at my soul. In eighteen years of school, college, and graduate school I never received a demerit. I believe in rules; without them I have always understood there would be chaos. I obey them. It is reasonable to expect inmates to be awakened by 6:00 A.M., perhaps even earlier. Standing assures the CO no one has committed suicide or died in her sleep. I find it childish and stupid not to obey a reasonable rule. Yet, programmed from childhood as I am to obey, I have now received nineteen Charge Sheets, one more contrived than the next, always for things that would and do go unnoticed in others. It is, I'm afraid, the privilege of notoriety.

I had asked that the two regular 11:00 P.M.–7:00 A.M. COs be witnesses for me to confirm that I am always standing at 6:00 A.M. and never refuse a direct order. They had both agreed to do so. But first the lieutenant called Dr. Prieto, who had signed a note saying the medication Mrs. Harris is taking is "very sedative" and could account for her not being fully awake at 6:00 A.M.

The doctor came on the phone; it was a conference call so that I could hear what he was saying. The lieutenant introduced herself and told him this was a hearing for Jean Harris, 81-G-98, and that the conversation was being recorded. The good doctor was obviously not pleased at being recorded. The lieutenant read his note, which stated the heart drugs plus antidepressant drug I take are "very sedative." "Oh," he sputtered, "that note, the nurse made me sign it." "You mean," said the lieutenant, "that you put your signature to something you don't believe is true?" "Oh, well, no. Read it back to me again." The lieutenant read the note again. "I think it's the 'very' that I object to." "You want it to read just sedative, not very sedative, is that correct?" "Yes, that's what I mean."

Then the fine doctor girded his loins and took the offensive. "What I mean is, I take some of that same medicine and I manage to get up and go to work and she can get up and go to work, too." A sad little man who lets nurses twist his arm was suggesting that I hadn't spent a lifetime being the first one to work and the last one to leave. I was enraged. I was just this side of a stroke. He had never even seen me. Maybe he doesn't know any more about medication than he knows about me. How dare he! So I did the worst possible thing. I burst into racking sobs. How could something as innocent as not springing from bed at the 6:00 A.M. count lead to a Tier Two trial, which is just below a Superintendent's trial, where being found guilty would not only remove one from the Honor Floor but could lead to solitary confinement? Straw under the fingernails would be about as appropriate.

"I think it's best if we postpone this hearing until you get yourself under control," the lieutenant said. "Oh, please, for Christ's sake, don't make me wait any longer to see what you're going to do to me," I sobbed. "Let me know now." She was trying to be decent and didn't want to make the whole performance any worse than it already was. "Well, go outside and wait, and I'll call you in later."

An hour went by. I sat on a broken couch in the Recreation Room trying to breathe and sobbing at the same time while women working out nearby on weights and other gym equipment stared or asked, "You okay, Jean?"

Finally, the lieutenant called me back. "I've decided you are not guilty on all three charges," she said. Two hours had gone by from the time the hearing began. More important, two hours of the lieutenant's time had gone by, a quarter of a well-paid day. Certainly there are better ways to put correctional money to work. And these hearings go on ad nauseam day after day after day. This was my nineteenth, and you would be hard put to find someone more respectful of rules than I am.

Love,
Jean

March 6, 1990

Dear Shana,

David came today to tell me that my sister Mary Margaret has had a heart attack and is in intensive care. Poor David. He always has to be the messenger who brings the bad news. He told me Mother had died. He told me Danny had died. I think he even told me Bill had died. He told me young Peter Kinney had died. I guess Marge told me Wilma had died.

There's something so unreal about sitting in a prison Visiting Room and hearing all this that makes it unreal, too. I don't feel all that I would feel outside. I won't really know they're all gone until I go out and they aren't there.

I called Virginia tonight, and she says Mary Margaret looks well and seems in good spirits and is going to be fine. I'm so glad Molly is nearby to be there for her. I can't do anything for anyone.

Love,
Jean

March 8, 1990

Dear Shana,

We're all so proud of Sister Elaine! Within the past six months she has been awarded a New York State commendation for her work in the Children's Center, the Eleanor Roosevelt Award for both the Children's Center summer program and her Providence Houses, and today a call came from the White House telling her that, out of 2,800 organizations and programs that were nominated for it, her Providence Houses are among nineteen that will be honored at the White House in April.

After all these years, I have finally produced something to give her to express my deep respect and affection. It's a cardigan, light brown alpaca with children of all races knitted into either side of the front opening and around the bottom front edge. In the back, around the edge, it says, "Joy is Unbreakable," which is part of the Children's Center motto:

"Joy is unbreakable, so it's perfectly safe in the hands of children." Needless to say, the sweater is a labor of love.

More love,
The Knitter—

March 11, 1990

Dear Shana

I watched two gray-flanneled businessmen being interviewed on television this evening. They assure me there's "big money" in addiction clinics today. They are just completing a luxurious $5 million building to be opened for that purpose. Fees will be $17,000 per month! That's what some working poor earn in just about three years, before taxes. Only former drug dealers could pay such a fee, but by golly, they'll have nothing but the best. A pregnant, indigent woman who wants to get off drugs has literally nowhere in the city of New York to go to get treatment. Fewer than a third of the people in prison in New York for drug-related crimes can get into drug programs even in prison. But if you happen to have $17,000 a month to spare, we know just the place for you.

Love,
Disgusted

March 20, 1990

Dear Shana,

Today was a lovely day in class, thanks to a young teacher in an inner-city school whom I will never meet and never forget. I always urge each new group of mothers to find out the name of their child's teacher and write to him or her. "Be honest with them about where you are, but most important, let them know how much you care. Ask how your child is doing and if there is anything you can do; even in here that will help the child's school performance. It matters so much to your child and the teacher to have you make the effort."

I rarely know who does or doesn't write. Lack of courage on a mother's part plays as large a role as lack of effort when they fail to write. Today Melba came to class clinging proudly to the response she had just received from her daughter's teacher. "Look at this. Look what I got. He thanked me. He thanked me for writing. And look how long it is." She held up two pages of a yellow legal-size pad, obviously well covered with writing. "He wrote all that?" another woman asked.

"Would you like to read it to us?" I asked. And she did. The letter said how much he appreciated her letter, that her daughter was such a nice little girl and doing quite well, with a little extra help in reading, and how he had told her what a fine letter her mother had written. It was so thoughtful and so respectful. The other mothers listened with rapt attention and a little envy. Two said, "I'm gonna mail my letter, too." That young teacher joins the ranks of life's small heroes in my book. If he does as much for his students' self-esteem as he did for Melba's, he's an educational treasure. It's the small things person to person that end up making the biggest difference.

Love,
Jean

March 22, 1990

Dear Shana,

I love Eugene McCarthy's comment to you about Michael taking Ivana Trump as a client. "It looks as though Michael has taken the high road." Maybe under all the glitz and tabloid trash she's really a good scout.

What do you think of this quote from my old friend A. N. Whitehead. "Style in its finest sense, is the last acquirement of the educated mind, it is also the most useful. It pervades the whole being. . . . Style is the ultimate morality of mind." Isn't it sad so many people think style is something you buy in a mall.

And speaking of style, I'm told that on Saturday afternoons around 2:00 P.M. someone sets up shop in his car out in the prison parking lot and sells T-shirts with various prison-related sayings on them. The joys of three hots and a cot moves well, but the hottest ticket has a picture of the electric chair on it with the question "How do you want it, regular or crispy?" They must tickle the mothers who come to visit their daughters. Who knows? Maybe they even buy some.

Love,
Jean

March 23, 1990

Dear Shana,

Lucia showed the class the movie *Do the Right Thing* today. I don't know whether it's this generation's version of *The Waste Land* or a modern Greek tragedy.

It rubs your nose in ugly realities and the blinding differences that age and cultures create in the eyes of the beholder.

I hope no one on the outside sits through that movie thinking it is an overstatement. It is so close to the mark it hurts to watch. I found it hard not to get up and leave. I guess it was the old game of chicken that kept me sitting there.

In the end, the character Sister-Mother spoke for me when she shrieked, "No! No! No!" as she watched the young people wildly destroying Sal's Pizza Parlor. Two of the young women watching with me murmured, "What's she yelling about?" A third one said, "I guess she's afraid her house will burn, too." A cry of pain for everyone there was something beyond their ken.

I'm grateful a black man made the movie. Had a white man made it, there would be movie houses burning all over the country. The women watched it quietly, thoughtfully. What was turning over in their minds, I don't know. One thing was clear from their quiet comments. They understood that in the end there were no winners.

I used to have a certain complacent, youthful disinterest in Greek tragedies. I thought they were exaggerated to the point of being foolish—at best, unconvincing. Now I live surrounded by them, immersed in them, even play an occasional lead role myself. And that movie is a Greek tragedy, too—even has a Greek chorus.

This afternoon, when the movie was over, I thought of Grosse Pointe and Dodie, who was afraid her daughter Sibley shouldn't go to see the movie *Gigi* for fear she would come away with the naughty notion that playing the role of mistress might be rather attractive. How did we all survive such innocence? Or perhaps the question is How will the world survive without us?

Jean

March 29, 1990

Dear Shana,

Virginia was collecting more vines this morning to make more of her lovely wreaths. She has finally gotten permission to send them out and is even permitted, I think, to sell some. She had gathered some vines on her way down to the clinic, and as she entered it, a young woman asked her, "Are you gonna make birds' nests outta that?" "No," she said, smiling. "People make bird houses, but birds build birds' nests." "They do?" the woman asked, not at all convinced. "Well, I still think you oughtta make some nests. There's a lotta birds around here, and they need nests."

How do you measure the emptiness of a life of, say, twenty-five or thirty years that has not somehow stumbled across the knowledge that birds build nests? Don't ask me who am I to look askance at another person's culture. Don't tell me a tree never grew in Brooklyn. Don't tell me they're street smart. Today I consider that an oxymoron. I've seen too many of the street smart, and heard them, too, to be moved by their much-touted smarts. They move in a vacuum, with pieces of life breaking off as they go, left as litter somewhere. They've been cheated, and they deserved better. But much of the cheating they've also done to themselves.

Love,
A sad lady

April 3, 1990

Dear Shana,

One of the little girls, the child of an inmate, who lives at My Mother's House, Sister Elaine's foster home for such children, slipped this note under the door of the nun who is her foster mother. "You are so beautiful. You are like a chocolate." I hate to think she may someday be calling people "motherfuckers," but sooner or later she'll hit the street, and she will. That's one of life's small tragedies that nobody takes very seriously.

I can't think of it without crying,

Jean

April 11, 1990

Dear Shana,

I started two new Red Cross courses this week, The Infant from Birth to Two. One group is made up of young mothers in the nursery who had not yet been offered the course. The other group is made up of pregnant women who've just recently come in. This time, I started the class discussing the importance of prenatal care and reading to them Superintendant Lord's memo about the additional foods pregnant women should be given by the prison kitchen. As usual, they were not being given any of it, and as usual, they were going to bed hungry.

The memo states:

Pregnant women must be given a *Minimum* of four (4) servings each of fresh fruit, fresh vegetables and dairy products every day. They should not eat as much bread/

cereal/carbohydrates as the other women. In order to accomplish this, I am granting permission for the pregnant women to take back fruit, vegetables, milk, cheese, eggs, etc., to their cells. You may be as generous as you can with these women, within reason and within the limits of their own individual consumption.

As new pregnant women come in, they are not made aware of the memo, and the prison kitchen makes a point of not telling them about it. In fact, even after the women know about it and ask for it, unless they are pregnant enough "to show," the kitchen says no.

Since most of the women eat dinner between four-thirty and five and are locked in for the night at ten, it isn't unusual to go to bed hungry. We go through this performance with each new class, so I give them a copy of the memo and recommend that they write a grievance if they aren't getting the food authorized for them.

I can think of nothing more shortsighted than to deny a pregnant woman adequate fruit, vegetables, and milk. The babies they are carrying have had enough strikes against them out on the street. The least we can do for them in here is make absolutely sure their mothers are getting adequate nutrition. Healthy babies are a gift to society, not an indulgence of the mother, even in prison.

Love,
Jean

April 14, 1990

Dear Shana,

I have heard about and read about brainwashing for years, but I have never met such a flagrant, egregious example of it as I met today. Mae is one of the women in my Red Cross Parenting Course. She is pregnant with her fourteenth child. She has twelve sons and one daughter. I can only imagine that what sent her to a parenting course was someone telling her she must. She is programmed to do as she is told.

She is thirty-eight years old. I suggested gently that a woman today does not have to have fourteen children. She quickly countered with "Ah don't believe in them abortions." The other women assured her abortion is not a woman's only option. I refrained from tossing in that old line from *Brother Rat:* "And a drugstore on every corner."

"Fourteen ain't so many. I was one of twenty-two. An' I started early," she said. "Had ma first baby when I was ten, by the man raped me."

"Your father permitted you at the age of ten to have the baby?"

"Oh, it was all right. We got married. Been married ever since."

"Your parents permitted you at the age of ten to marry a man who raped you?"

"It was all my fault, Jean. I done it. I was a real sexy kid at ten. I was askin' for it. It was all my fault."

"Mae, when a ten-year-old child is raped, it is not the fault of the child. It is the fault of the bastard who raped her."

"Yes, I calls him a bastard, too, but we still together. Whenever he come around, we has another baby." There is a dichotomy in her use of the word "rape" and her insistence that the whole thing was her fault. We don't go into that.

Mae raised her children in South Carolina, near her family's house, where, incidentally, she also worked in the same factory for fifteen years. Her one run for freedom was a year ago when she took off for a weekend with a woman friend from New York City and was quickly caught up in a crack raid at her friend's house. She has a one-to-three sentence. It may well prove to be the best rest she's had in twenty years, not to mention three meals a day she doesn't have to cook for sixteen people before she leaves for work.

She is affable and indulgent as we talk about the responsibilities of "parenting" and assures us her children are all "just fine." "Only one give me trouble is they father." Her eighteen-year-old daughter, whom we especially ask about, "Don't want no children, hasn't got none, and works for the airlines." We're all happy to hear it.

Love,
Jean

April 19, 1990

Dear Shana,

Imogene got fifteen to life as her sentence. She paid her lawyer $4,600 to handle her appeal. His $4,600 worth of services consisted of telling her, "I find absolutely no basis upon which you can appeal."

Imogene then went to the prison law library every single night for a year and with a little help from a legal aid lawyer wrote her own appeal. She just won the appeal, by a unanimous decision. There was no one to tell her she won it. She read it in the law journal that she had gotten in the habit of reading while she worked on her appeal. Her lawyer sent her a letter this week saying he was so sorry he'd been wrong. No money came back with the apology. It's the first time she had heard from him in over two years.

Jean

April 22, 1990

Dear Shana,

The excitement of the day was the theft in 121B by one of the inmates of a CO's wallet, ID, and badge. The CO was new, still on probation, and I'm told may lose her job. Having an officer's badge and ID loose in a top-security prison is a definite no-no. The women in 121B were locked down, en masse, since they live in little cubicles that can't be locked individually. Their cubicles were torn apart, lockboxes up-ended, mattress rolled up and tossed in the walkways between rows of cubicles. Nothing was found.

Word of such a search soon spreads over the whole facility, and soon an air of excitement begins to pervade the whole place. As it builds up, just about everyone is rooting for the guilty party. For most, the lovely satisfaction of seeing the administration with egg on its face is worth whatever inconvenience a lock-in causes. If they don't find the missing stuff by tomorrow, we'll probably all be locked in.

Love,
Jean

April 24, 1990

Dear Shana,

I was wrong. They didn't lock us all down until today, Tuesday. Now we are indeed locked in. The chances of finding on Tuesday something that was stolen on Sunday are slim indeed. It could have gone out in two mails, it could have gone out in the trash, it could be lying under a rock somewhere, who knows. How long we'll be locked in, I don't know, but they've canceled all afternoon classes and college classes tonight. I guess the purpose of the show is to say, "We are not amused."

When something may have been stolen by a CO or other staff member, the reaction is always the same. "Yeah, well, how do I know you even had one in the first place." A week ago someone broke into the Children's Center office with a crowbar and stole a case of white jackets that had been donated for us to give to teenage inmate children. It was logistically impossible for an inmate to have taken them. It was broken into at night, and inmates are not permitted there after three-thirty except to clean, and then only with CO supervision. Two weeks ago, a box of fruit sent to me was lying on the floor of the Package Room empty when I came to receive it. The CO in the Package Room told me, "The fruit fairy took it." He found the thought so irresistibly cute he repeated himself three times. "The fruit fairy took it." Inmates are allowed in the Package Room only on rare occasions, and then only in the presence of COs. Many things disappear from the Package Room. If you complain or grieve it, you are left with the distinct impression that if you continue to complain they'll take away the privilege of getting any packages at all. A little like the protections racket. The inmate always loses. Now something of theirs is missing, and they're going bananas.

When you do business with people like this long enough, you can understand why many inmates take a certain amount of pleasure in "getting back some of their own." Of course, there are some decent guards here. But there are some decent inmates, too. They do not learn the lessons society would have them learn by watching too closely what goes on in here.

Love,
Jean

April 25, 1990

Dear Shana,

Three days of lockdowns, cell searches, accusations, and general chaos ended today because the CO who had reported her wallet, ID, and badge stolen from her coat pocket discovered she had put them all in someone else's coat. The CO whose coat it was in went off for three days and either didn't discover or didn't bother to call and report that he had them all in his coat pocket.

The Tuesday that the entire facility was locked down, even the civilian staff, secretaries, teachers, and all were drafted into working overtime to carry food to 850 inmates, lunch and dinner. I wonder what that unnecessary lockdown cost the poor taxpayers.

Several weeks ago we had a similar crisis when a case of medication and a case of hypodermic needles were missing from the storehouse. This time the search went on all night, with the Superintendent at the helm of the search. The few inmates who have access to the storehouse were searched inch by inch and their cells were taken apart. In the morning it was discovered that one of the cases had never been delivered. The other had been shipped back the morning before because it was the wrong order. I'm glad I don't have to run this place, I'd probably make a lot of the same mistakes out of sheer exhaustion and inevitable paranoia.

Love,
Lucky

April 30, 1990

Dear Shana,

The marketplace of ideas, in here as well as outside, doesn't handle as many useful items as it should. To do so would quickly cause the stall keepers to be labeled racist, however good their intentions. In here we aren't brave enough to deal in things most of the women don't want to hear. But then neither is Congress, the president, or the media. Truth is not a big vote-getter, once you've figured out what it is. Though over the long haul I'm sure it's more loving than putting people down by lying to them.

I know some of my well-meaning, and I think useful, homilies do not always fall on grateful ears in here and are not what I'm told is currently called "PC," politically correct. I tell them, "We live the way we speak. Your children will, too." "It's good practice to get to class on time. People who don't get to work on time soon lose their jobs." "You will be the most important teacher your children will ever have. They will go off to school quickly, but how they will enjoy the experience, and succeed at it is very much in your hands." "Turn off the television set. Too many hours of it are damaging to all children, but especially to black children." "How do you feel about drug users having babies?" etc., etc.

One of the ladies chose a very civil way to express her reservations about me. I still don't know who she is, but I admire her. She found a picture and taped it on the door that connects our classroom to the Parenting Office. It's a picture of a white woman who could be my mother, hairdo circa 1918. She is attractive, wearing a long strand of pearls and fingering them casually. The color of the picture is a grayish brown, almost sepia, and looks as though it may have come from a very old magazine. Across the top is printed: "In any field one has to define and redefine one's own prejudices." The words are those of the magazine but obviously express what the message was meant to be for me.

I have the greatest respect for whoever put it there, and I read it each day as I open the classroom door, a useful reminder.

It isn't easy to be sure of anything anymore, but teachers, I believe, should have a few convictions they cling to if only to give their students something from which to spring. You can't take a running jump into life from a bowl of pudding.

Well, can you?

Jean

May 1, 1990

Dear Shana,

Pat and the Care Givers took the babies out in the fresh air this afternoon. And the air is fresh here—a true plus for all of us. The temperature was almost ninety, but every child, from two months to twelve months, had on shoes, stockings, undershirt, diapers, and dress or shirt and pants. One baby only was lying on a blanket, happily gurgling in nothing but shirt and diaper. His mother came back from her class and stopped to pick up the child, took one look at it, and screamed hysterically, "Oh, ma Gawd! My baby ain't got no clothes on. He ain't got nothin' on. Who done that? I'm writin' this up. I'm grievin' this, you see if I don't. Who done this to my baby?"

We have begged the mothers not to put shoes on the babies for the nine years I have been here, and before, too, I'm sure. But putting shoes on babies and dressing them to the nines is a cultural thing that isn't about to change in here—certainly not on my say-so. It is a matter of mother's pride. And since the women cannot get all dressed up themselves, the baby has the additional burden of having to look good in the mother's place. "I may not have much, but I got nice things for my baby." I said one day in desperation, "Ladies, the prince of Wales, when his mother the queen played with him under the trees on a hot summer day, was, I'm sure, out there in shirt and diaper." Someone called out, "Who gives a shit?" I use a different tack today—simply plead for the baby's comfort. "Think how good it feels to you to run around in your bare feet." The answer came back: "Ah never runs in bare feet—it give ya diseases."

Love,
The Barefoot Contessa

May 3, 1990

Dear Shana,

I don't know how many miles it is from here to Long Island Sound, but obviously it isn't too far for sea gulls to visit us regularly. They land on the roof of the dining hall, which is right outside our Recreation Room windows, and join the mourning doves there. There's a pure white dove that perches there from time to time and a magnificent sea gull, much the largest of them all, with a pure white tail that looks like velvet. The others have tails of black and white or gray and white. I've seen only one with a pure white tail—a splendid fellow indeed.

There's something about seeing the birds swoop in and out that leaves you suspecting that if you don't think you're a prisoner, then maybe you aren't one. The trick is just to keep looking up.

Love,
Jean

May 4, 1990

Dear Shana,

Today they took the stones away from around Virginia's garden, per the deputy superintendent of security. Now people can and will walk all over the flowers. The stones have been there for four years and served their purpose without causing any harm. It's difficult to walk ten feet on this prison campus without stepping over stones and small rocks—even big ones. For more than three years the main walkway leading to all of the living units was covered with loose cobblestones until it suddenly occurred to someone that this was "terribly dangerous" and tar was applied.

The Children's Center was broken into—at night, when it couldn't have been by inmates—and we still don't know who did it. But by God, they've taken care of the stones around Virginia's garden. Do something, even if it isn't needed. That way no one can say you aren't busy.

How I long for a garden far away from here where no one can destroy it—where no one would want to destroy it. But gardens are for dreaming, Shana. For now, gardens are only for dreaming.

Love,
Jean

May 5, 1990

Dear Shana,

Joan came to visit today and brought me a bunch of daffodils. "I was so proud of myself, because I remembered that you can't have glass containers, so I found a plastic one and put a little water in it to keep the flowers fresh. When I reached the prison gate, the officer told me I couldn't bring 'that thing' in. I told him, 'But it's plastic; plastic is allowed.' He said, 'Well, all right, but you can't bring in that water.' "

Alice came yesterday, bringing my groceries as usual. Salad material is always at the top of my list, but today the celery wasn't allowed in because she had cut off the leafy tops. "You can't bring in stuff that's been altered," she was told, and she had to take the altered celery back to Vermont.

Sleep well tonight, my friend, with an untroubled mind. There's no dangerous celery abroad in the land, not in New York State; anyway, not tonight.

Love,
Jean

May 9, 1990

Dear Shana,

While Carmen was in prison, her daughter Mavis was in foster care. She is just thirteen, a special child, resilient, loving, an earnest student, a child you feel sure will "make it." You wish good things for her.

Things seemed to break well for Carmen when she went out on parole. She got a job; she got an apartment in the Bronx; she got Mavis back to live with her. They finally were a family again. They had each other.

Three evenings ago, two men broke into Carmen's apartment and told her, "We're looking for Mavis, but you'll do." They beat her unmercifully, raped her, and left her bleeding on the floor.

The building where Carmen had found her new home is

rife with drug dealers. Mavis was known to have reported some of them to the police. When you want to stay alive in the drug world, you don't talk to the police. The rape is only a small sample of what could follow if they were to stay in the apartment. Carmen was taken to the hospital; her few belongings were moved by the police to another apartment, where her address will not be known. Sister Tisa went at once to get Mavis and take her back to the foster home she runs. Sister Elaine went at once to the hospital to see Carmen. "You know, Sister," she said. "Prison wasn't the prison. This is the prison. I was never afraid at Bedford. Out here that's all I am is afraid. I'm afraid for Mavis, afraid for me, always afraid. I can't afford to run away, and I'm afraid to stay." If anyone wants to know about victims, I can tell them about victims. Sometimes I feel as though it's the only thing I know about anymore—just wall-to-wall victims.

Sadly,
Jean

May 12, 1990

Dear Shana,

Until yesterday Loretta lived in the prison nursery with her four-month-old baby boy. Then she had a fight with a CO, was moved off the nursery floor, and her baby had to go home. A quick call was made to her mother. "Ma, you gotta come and get the baby." More than one mother has received that call over the years, and though she may have planned to take the baby when it turned a year old, with a few hours' notice she now has to put her own life on hold, hop the train from Grand Central, and pick up the baby, together with all its paraphernalia.

She hasn't a car, of course, and she arrives with little idea of how she will get baby and boxes of baby stuff home on a train and two buses. Sister Elaine often ends up driving Grandmother home. As far as I know, no one else in here has ever volunteered. The closest they come to it is calling Sister.

As they drove along yesterday, Sister could hear Grandmother Bertha laughing quietly to herself. "Mmmm mmm. Look at me. Just look at me, gettin' a ride home. Minister said to me Sunday, 'Bertha, it ain't right you doin' good for so many others and so much bad luck comin' your way.' Well, today's my lucky day. Here I am gettin' a ride home." A little later, chuckling to herself again, "Wouldn't you know it. My daughter give me a hair appointment for tomorrow for a Mother's Day gift. I haven't had my hair fixed for years. Now I can't go."

Sister said, "Well, you ought to go. Get a sitter for a little while and go."

"No indeed. I'm going to take the baby to the doctor tomorrow and have him checked all over."

"Did you give any thought to foster care for the child, Bertha?"

"Oh, no, Sister. I would never do that. You takes care of your own. You takes care of your own."

It rained hard all during the drive, but as they turned off on the little side street that was the entrance to her project apartment, the rain was coming down in sheets. How to get out of the car with the baby and all its belongings? They sat for a moment or two, and suddenly Sister said, "Never mind. I know what we'll do." She backed the car up for a running start, drove up over the curb, and right up to the door.

Bertha laughed as though it were the funniest thing she'd ever seen. A neighbor came down to help her and clapped his hands, calling, "Right on! Right on!" She waved good-bye to

Sister as she stood in the doorway, holding the baby, her head thrown back, still laughing. It was a homecoming they would tell the child about in the years to come. It might have been the luckiest day of his life.

Love,
Jean

May 16, 1990

Dear Shana,

I girded my loins, or whatever it is one girds to feel brave, and wrote to Barbara Bush today. It's so important for us to get a child care bill through Congress, and soon. I decided it wouldn't hurt for one more voice to be heard in its behalf, even if that voice belongs to a prisoner. I've written my congressmen. Although I have lost my right to cast a vote, I can still write a letter.

I know Barbara Bush is not an Eleanor Roosevelt (that is not meant to be judgmental one way or the other), which probably makes for more peace and smiles around the family dinner table, but I'm sure she cares deeply about children, and she knows education doesn't start in high school, which many American educators still find hard to accept. I don't know why.

It doesn't take long to write a letter. Imagine how much difference individuals could have made if they'd written Nixon in 1971, when the first child care bill was passed. But Phyllis Schlafly and her crew wrote the letters instead, and Nixon vetoed it. It could have been as important to this country as opening up China, possibly more so. Hard to compare convincingly the nation of China and a bunch of little kids, but uneducated, troubled kids have had more to do with where the country is today than China has had. It still isn't really "open," anyway.

I ended my letter to Barbara Bush with a simple but to-the-point allegorical tale I first read in the Urban League's annual publication, *The State of Black America*. See if you like it.

One summer day two men were fishing from a boat in a briskly running stream. Suddenly they began to see babies in the water floating downstream past the boat, struggling and crying and trying to survive. One of the men in the boat quickly jumped into the water and began to catch as many babies as he could, tossing them into the boat to save them from drowning. Meanwhile his companion jumped over the other side of the boat and began to swim to shore. Seeing this, the first man shouted, "Wait. Where are you going? Help me," as he continued to try to catch the babies and get them into the boat. The second person kept swimming to shore but paused to respond, "You keep trying to save as many as you can, but I'm going upstream to stop that person from throwing them into the water in the first place."

By this late date in our history every child who is eligible for it should have a place in a Head Start program. It's now only one in four who can get in. And Head Start should be run by qualified teachers with at least a B.A. and a salary at least as high as that of a prison guard. I'm told the head of the Head Start program in one of our affluent neighboring towns earns less than $9,000 a year. She holds down two other jobs to pay her bills. The guards at this prison start at $25,000. If that doesn't indicate a skewed national value system, what could? The guards can retire on more than Head Start teachers earn in a year. And Head Start teachers don't have a retirement program. You can teach fifteen years in one of them and then head for a public shelter to spend your golden years.

You give so many talks in the course of a year. Thump the drum for a child care bill whenever you can.

Love,
Jean

May 18, 1990

Dear Shana,

I read in the papers that Ivan Boesky is a very bad boy because he paid someone to do his laundry for him while he was in prison. How silly. He's a very bad boy, but not for that reason. It is common practice in prisons for the have-nots to seek employment from the haves. They vie for such jobs because it's the only way some of them can buy themselves cigarettes or shaving cream or an occasional candy bar.

Prices in our prison commissary have doubled since I came here, but prison pay is the same. For those who get the maximum, it's a $7.76 per week, but few earn more than $5.00 per week. Furthermore, mistakes and omission of payments are not uncommon, and it can be a hard struggle to get back a few dollars owed.

When I first arrived here, week after week my prison sheets failed to come back from the prison laundry. I was forever going down to the Sergeant's office and begging for a sheet and a pillow case. Finally, a lieutenant told me, "Mrs. Harris, you've got to learn about jailing. If you want your laundry back, get to know someone who works in the laundry, give her a couple of packs of cigarettes each week, and you'll find your laundry will always show up."

I have made it a practice not to pay anyone to do my prison tasks, first because it isn't my style; second, because I needed the money, too, to keep up our bingo project with the ladies of the mental ward; and third, because I knew when I arrived everyone was waiting for me to assume the role the media had given me, "Queen Jean." I've probably washed as many floors as any woman in here, but I'm sure they would never believe it. The only task I have paid someone else to do happened recently: emptying the large garbage cans and carrying the contents two city blocks (the equivalent of) to the nearest Dumpster. I couldn't lift the bags.

Today they have made washing and ironing such a task that people with money gladly pay others to do it for them. The prison laundry is a risk, so women send only their state issue to it, nothing they value. I had a small yellow rug that I sent two weeks ago. It was washed with all the dark green clothes and came back a vomitous shade of dirty mustard green. I tossed it.

There are washing machines and dryers on each floor, but we are forbidden to use them. There is one large sink in the kitchen where one can wash things by hand, when it isn't filled with greasy pans. There's a second sink, too, but that has been clogged for many weeks and may not be fixed for another year or two. There is one iron for sixty women, and we're fortunate enough to have it because one of the women stole it from the place she works. When I need to iron something, I stand by my door just before it opens at six-thirty and run for it. Occasionally, I get there first. More often there are three women ahead of me. To get your turn, you must of course sit in a chair right next to the ironing board (propped up on two chairs). To leave for five minutes means ten women have moved in ahead of you in the line. "I told Ethel she could have my place, and Winnie Mae was right after me, and she'd already told Big Feet that she could be next, etc., etc., etc." What could easily be made simple is inevitably made compli-cated and a ready source of anger and frustration. If we break an iron too fast, we should be charged seventy-five cents a piece to buy another one. But we aren't allowed to buy one.

If the seventy-five cents had to be charged too frequently, we might even learn to be more careful with the iron we have. Sixty women on one iron, however, does cause it to age quickly.

The washing machine nonsense only teaches cheaters to cheat more. It doesn't save water at all, though that is the reason given us for not using it. It's just one more mindless rule. If Boesky's prison is anything like this one, it isn't too hard to understand why he paid someone to do his laundry. The lieutenant would call it "good jailing" even though it's against the rules.

Love,
The Harried Laundress

May 22, 1990

Dear Shana,

I was the last one out of the Visiting Room today, and by the time I had been strip-searched, it was almost four o'clock. I was afraid I'd be caught in the count and have to sit in traffic until the count cleared—sometimes until five o'clock. I hadn't a book or knitting with me, and the thought of sitting for a whole hour with absolutely nothing to do weighed heavily.

Suddenly a captain walked by and said, "No reason for you to sit there for a long time. I'll take you back." It isn't a captain's job to escort prisoners, so I thanked her profusely, and we started up the hill. We made an incongruous couple, two old ladies whose paths would never have crossed if the world hadn't come to an end for one of them—two old ladies who happen cordially to dislike one another.

We had taken only a few steps when the captain started to sing, "What a day this has been, what a rare mood I'm in, why it's almost like being in love." At "There's a smile on my face for the whole human race," I joined her in song. We could have been holding a milk pail between us like Jack and Jill. As I think of it, I have to laugh.

Love,
Jean

May 23, 1990

Dear Shana,

As you walk down the stairs by the staff dining hall and you look to the left, you'll see Virginia's other garden. The irises are in bloom right now, but daylilies and wild phlox and a few wild roses will come next. Gardens are not encouraged, here, though of course they should be. They are not only not encouraged; they are forbidden except for twenty-six women in Fiske Honor Cottage. What an empty, counterproductive gesture to make growing your own food and creating beauty a privilege for 26 out of 850 women, who know so little about beauty or how to take care of themselves. The place should be alive with flowers and women who take pride in them. There are flowers in one other place, bordering the walkway up to the prison, where prisoners don't go. Our walkways, in between maintenance tours, are strewn with plastic cups, cigarette butts, banana peels, and other garbage. Thank God for Virginia's garden.

Love,
Jean

June 1, 1990

Dear Shana,

I fell down again on the hill today and scraped a hole in the new pants I was given when I tore a hole in my last pair of new pants. The pair I've worn for six years are still intact, faded and worn, but I manage to remain upright in them. Kind people ran from every corner to help me up and make sure I was all right, all of them insisting that I should go at once and have a doctor or nurse check me. I assured them I have been scraping the same left knee for sixty years and it's quite accustomed to handling the whole thing by itself.

I'm afraid my age makes people very jumpy about me. A CO came rushing up to me and wrote down my name and number and the fact that I chose not to go to the hospital. This is so if I drop dead in two days they can wash their hands of any responsibility. I don't blame them for that. This is a litigious bunch of women, and you have to keep covering your tracks.

If dear old friends in their eighties were not still looking good, playing golf, traveling, and coming to visit, I would not awake each day with any sense of optimism about tomorrow. I wouldn't give odds that I will live to get out of here, but I certainly don't tell them that in here.

Love,
Shaky but still going strong

June 7, 1990

Dear Shana,

Glenda lives on 113C and has a lover who lives on 112A. Tippy lives on 112A and has a lover who lives on 113C. The two got together in the gym Friday night and decided the only solution to their problem was to switch cells. Since the prison is filled with young COs in training who are falling over one another, scratching their heads, trying to figure out what their job entails over and above locking and unlocking doors, it seemed a good time to try. The women switched identification cards, then Tippy headed for Glenda's cell and Glenda headed for Tippy's. It was all so simple they might have been starting a new prison game. Until Sunday morning.

Glenda came out into the Recreation Room in a bathrobe just as a sergeant who knows her came on the floor. "Glenda, what are you doing up here in that getup?" he asked. The young CO in charge spoke up. "Her name's not Glenda, it's Tippy." "The hell it is," the sergeant replied. The jig was up, but like so many jigs, it was fun while it lasted. The four lovers are presently in lock in their respective cells. The road to true love is usually bumpy. Just in case you didn't know.

Love,
Jean

June 10, 1990

Dear Shana,

Mary Margaret will be seventy on the twentieth of June, and I've spent my spare time this week making her a collage birthday card. It's filled with reminiscences of our childhood summers. Apparently I've reached that point in my life that I'd once only heard about when the details of long gone yesterdays are clearer in my mind than what I had for breakfast this morning. It's rather a nice arrangement for someone in here.

As the number of pages in the card grew, I found myself thinking of things that hadn't crossed my mind in sixty years;

how we swung on the vines in Mr. Ashton's woods, walked for miles up the beach and tried to climb the cliff in our bare feet, or collected pretty stones and then built jewelry stores in the sand and sold them to each other. Or how we shopped at the general store in Morpeth and stared at Cooney Smith and whispered that "he sucks raw eggs."

Gym shoes cost $1.95 and were all alike except they came in black and white and you always wore white ones and the kids who wore the black ones were considered sort of eccentric—"them" not "us." Faded blue denims got that way because your older sister wore them first. You hadn't a clue whose father had the most money, because it was during the depression and everyone was broke. The only thing I can remember silently envying another child was the extra thick slices of bologna the Kolb kids had in their picnic sandwiches. I found out years later that their father was in the wholesale meat business and bologna was what they had most of. We dressed up in our mother's clothes, and we collected sea gull feathers and painted our faces and were Indians. We walked to the haunted house and tested our "guts" by climbing to the top of the rusty windmill that stood beside it, and we picnicked at "the wreck" of an old rumrunner that had plied whiskey between Windsor, Ontario, and Detroit, Michigan, one time too many.

Today we'd call it a sheltered life, but it wasn't sheltered then at all. Grown-ups minded their business, and we were permitted the lovely luxury of minding ours without being warned about being snatched by crazed killers or having babies while we were still in grammar school or warned not to play with machine guns and heroin. The only caveat I can remember my mother giving us before she set us free for the summer was "Don't swim out too far," a useful piece of advice that covers just about everything, if you let it.

Maybe the downward journey began the year the Lindbergh baby was kidnapped and the entire country still had the good grace to be shocked by shocking things, and even things less than shocking. I'm glad we were alive and young when the entire country worried over whether Rhett Butler should say "damn" on the silver screen.

Frankly, Scarlett, today nobody gives a damn.

Love,
Jean

June 12, 1990

Dear Shana,

Precious graduates from college this Friday. I have watched her work through many of her courses. She is a conscientious and able student. For her, Friday is an important day, and rightly so.

Her daughter and grandson, who live upstate, are coming for the occasion, an expensive trip for them but worth the sacrifices. Precious had asked if one of the prison trailers would be available over graduation so her family could stay overnight and be sure to be on time for graduation. She was called down this morning and told that due to a cancellation a trailer visit was available to her. Just one problem. "Per the captain, you can have the trailer visit or go to your graduation, but you can't do both. We can't be bothered sending a CO down to the trailers to escort you to the gym." It is at most a four-minute walk from the trailers to the gym.

One of the staff has now offered to take her daughter and grandson for the night and bring them to graduation. The captain and her teeny, tiny brain be damned.

Love,
Jean

June 13, 1990

Dear Shana,

A friend sent me clippings from three powerful articles by David Remnick in the *Washington Post* about life in Russia today. The picture is so grim, with so much suffering, it makes me look gratefully at my clean, relatively comfortable cage and ask again the impossible question "What's fair?" Should American criminals be shoveled into the Russian gulag or even into a fast-fading Soviet village and the honest peasants, at least reasonably honest peasants, be moved into the relative comfort of an American prison? If the exchange could be made, I'm sure many American citizens would support it. I've heard and read the suggestion that we stop building prisons and establish our own Devil's Island "somewhere in the Aleutians." "Let 'em survive the best way they can." Australia turned out pretty well, but I wouldn't want to be part of a new experiment.

I wonder who ever started the myth of fairness. The law has nothing to do with fairness, and neither have judges, and neither has life in general. I don't know what poor old blindfolded, arm-tired Justice has to do with it, either. I think she put the blindfold on herself just to have a little peace and quiet.

Best,
Jean

June 15, 1990

Dear Shana,

Today was graduation day at Bedford Hills, unquestionably the nicest day of the year in here, because the accent is on accomplishments, not mistakes. The women look pretty, and they look proud; perhaps that's why they look pretty. Their families come to cheer them on, someone important like a member of the New York City Council gives the graduation address, and a very nice lunch is served to everyone when the ceremonies are over and Father Gorman has given the benediction. Father Gorman is easily the most colorful member of the procession in his flowing red doctoral robe. With the cap rakishly over one eye, he looks very much like Henry VIII.

Most of the women were being honored for completing a high school equivalency course. I was there to honor Precious, who was one of nine women receiving a bachelor's degree from Mercy College, which teaches all the college courses offered here. Judy Clark was the valedictorian with a 4.0 average, the second woman from Bedford to graduate with that record in the past three years. Her speech was short and showed great restraint, considering her strong convictions and the terrible pressure she is always under. She said:

This is the largest graduating class we have ever had at Bedford. Among us are women who developed expertise in foster-care policies and emotional issues in order to counsel mothers trying to maintain their family bonds; among us are women who studied law and helped their peers and themselves to pursue and even win their appeals. Some of us worked together to develop a program of peer education, counseling, and support to meet the needs of our community in the AIDS epidemic. We have women who came into this prison as young teens, who had to grow up and achieve maturity the hard way, and who now work with and share their experience with young women just coming into the system. We have women who are getting ready to take their diplomas and leave this institution, to begin new careers and new lives, and there are those of us who are clamoring to continue our education—working to institute a master of social work program here at Bedford—because we need to develop our expertise and professionalism. . . . We are serious and dedicated. . . .

I don't live on the same floor as Judy does, but women who do tell me she has a large picture on the front of her cell door of a gentle-eyed man holding a beautiful grinning young child. Under it she has printed a few lines from a Langston Hughes poem. I don't remember it exactly. It's the one about holding fast to our dreams because without them life is incomplete, like a bird with a broken wing that cannot fly. She ended her talk with a hopeful "We have taken up our wings and we have begun to fly." It sounds like Judy, and it describes more than a few other women here.

This is the other side of prison women that I don't write about enough.

Love,
Jean

June 20, 1990

Dear Shana,

I heard from Barbara Bush today. Say what you will, it's exciting to receive a letter from the White House. It's a funny feeling to think an old Smith girl is now a piece of history, but indeed she is.

I don't feel at all the same way about Nancy Reagan, though they were both at Smith while I was there. But Nancy is so unlike the many Smith women I know, salt-of-the-earth types. Slim and carefully coiffed she is; salt of the earth, no. But she, too, is a piece of history, and now part of the college's history as well.

Barbara's letter was warm, friendly, and short. She said she had read my books, was interested in our work here, and ended with "I'll do my best to head upriver." Good lady.

Fondly,
Jean

June 25, 1990

Dear Shana,

Maria's son Lenny was married to Ann, a pretty, young schoolteacher, on Saturday. Lenny plays sax in a band and teaches music at a large public high school. His kids won "best in the state" last month at a statewide competition. His younger brother, Anthony, who is in his second year of law school, was best man. Maria, of course, couldn't be there, and it has been hurting her for months. Her sons adore her, and the feeling is mutual.

But Maria has been taking part in the festivities in every way that she can, making favors for all the guests at a shower, addressing all the wedding invitations in her handsome script, making sweaters for the bride and groom, and working every minute of her own time to earn money to send the bride and groom a wedding gift.

Maria's brother is a priest in Rome. He came to perform the wedding ceremony, bringing with him the pope's blessing. Another brother and several nieces also came from Italy for the ceremony. On Sunday, yesterday, both brothers, the bride and groom, and Anthony came to visit her in one of the prison trailers. The bride and groom dressed in their wedding finery, and many pictures were taken with Maria, by a staff person.

Maria had asked for permission for her son to bring in a dress she could wear for the pictures. Absolutely not! We wanted her to look like the mother of the groom, if only for the pictures. She ended up wearing a light pink silk robe that my brother had sent me from the Far East, arranged as a long skirt, a friend's fancy blouse, and a string of opera-length "pearls" that someone had sent with some odds and ends of things for bingo prizes but which we weren't allowed to use. I haven't seen the pictures yet, but Maria seemed happy with the total effect.

They all spent the night together in the trailer, talking away the hours. At 5:30 A.M., Anthony left to get back to his job in the district attorney's office in Philadelphia, both brothers had a leisurely breakfast with their sister, and by ten the visit was all over. The bride and groom leave tonight for their honeymoon in Italy, where they will visit Lenny's grandmother and many cousins and aunts and uncles. By then he'll have the pictures developed to take with him. The pictures are very important. Maria's eighty-six-year-old mother does not know that she is in prison, with a sentence of twenty-five to life, and Maria wants her to die in peace. So do I.

Love,
Jean

June 27, 1990

Dear Shana,

More from the Looney Tunes Department. Yesterday there was a facilitywide fire drill. We hardly ever have fire drills—I've been in four in nine and a half years—but now we're having them frequently because the administration hopes to make this an accredited prison. The trouble with yesterday's drill was that alarms were rung only here and there in a few buildings and the ones that were rung were so short many people figured it was just something going off by mistake, which happens all the time. Consequently, if you became part of the drill, it was pure happenstance.

I left work and returned to my housing unit apparently right in the middle of it. At the iron grill leading to 14 Lobby I called out, "On the gate," for the CO to come and open it. No one came. I called out again. Still no one came. Three other women arrived at the gate. One called out; another kicked the gate and yelled. Eleven minutes went by, and we stood there in the tunnel locked between 13 Lobby and 14 Lobby. Finally a CO came. "Hold your horses," he said. "I couldn't let you out. We're in the middle of a fire drill." Fortunately, the tunnel wasn't on fire. Someday there will be a tragedy here, not a cartoon.

Love,
Jean

June 30, 1990

Dear Shana,

Prison often (more than often?) brings out the worst in people, and tonight I certainly let it do so. I keep thinking of Mother saying, "We're just as big as the things that make us angry," which tonight makes me the size of a cashew, or maybe even a peanut.

I was brought some gifts by a friend today, fresh flowers and a tin of nuts. At the prison gate she was told, "You can't bring in that can. You'll have to empty the can into a paper bag." She opened the hermetically sealed can as directed and emptied the nuts into a brown paper bag. When I went to the Package Room to pick them up, I was told, "You can't have the nuts because they aren't in a sealed container." This didn't concern me at all. "My son Jim is coming tomorrow. Just give the nuts to him."

"Yeah, fine. He'll get 'em."

"I want to sign the sheet and put his name on it so he'll be sure to get them."

"Don't you know the rules by now? You don't sign nothin' unless you want it to be thrown away."

"That isn't true. I've signed hundreds of those papers. How else can you know which package goes where?"

"I'm tellin' you you don't sign no paper and your son'll get the nuts."

"I'd like to see them and have them labeled for him."

"You're not seein' 'em and I'm busy, so get outta my face and go back where you come from."

"I have the right to see them and be sure they go to the right person."

"Well, I'm tellin' you you're not signin' nothin' and you're not seein' no nuts and get outta here."

"Then I'd like to see a sergeant."

"You wanna see a sergeant, go find one."

I went to the CO who had escorted us to the Package Room and asked, "Will you please get me a sergeant. This woman is deliberately lying to me." "Oh, she's in charge," he said. "I can't go over her head." "Then please come with me and hear what the woman is saying." By this time she was yelling, "I'm tellin' you your son'll get 'em and you aren't signin' no paper."

At that point I went back and sat down. Two minutes later, the woman called me back to the Package Room window. "Harris, come back here. Yer package went out with your visitors. We give it back to them."

"Who told you that?" I asked. She waved her arm around an empty Package Room. "Do you see anyone in here?"

"No. That's why I asked who told you."

"I knew it all the time."

"And you knew it when you assured me Jim would be given them? I'm going to grieve this."

"Fine. Be sure you spell my name right—H-O-W-A-R-D."

Next day I called the friend to see if the nuts had been returned to her. "No, they weren't," she said.

This is not an unusual day's rehabilitation program by a correction officer at Bedford Hills Correctional Facility. How silly of me not to let 'em steal the nuts and be done with it. There's a holier-than-thou quality in me that causes me much pain. As I reread the above, I sound a little like Captain Queeg and his damn strawberries. My mother would not be proud.

Love,
Queeg

July 3, 1990

Dear Shana,

Someday some bright young man or woman is going to reinvent the old Royal typewriter with nothing on it but the alphabet, the numbers from 0 to 9, and the basic punctuation marks. And people like me, of whom there are more than IBM dreams, will buy them.

Love,
Jean

July 4, 1990

Dear Shana,

There's a new CO working in traffic from time to time. It's a woman, but you have to look twice to be sure. She looks like a man, male haircut and deep voice. Her one nod to a feminine touch is long fingernails, painted black. She has added several of her own touches to the strip search, even a few the Witch of Endor has missed.

"Lift up your arm," a deep voice says. "I want to check your armpits." But her *pièce de résistance* is "the squat." "Now squat and cough," she says, and as she says it, she bends over into the shape of a croquet wicket and looks directly into the anus.

"You really are revolting," I said to her. She didn't seem to take offense at all. I shall think of her always as the Anus and Armpit Queen. How could she help but make us all better citizens?

Love,
Jean

July 7, 1990

Dear Shana,

I've just taken a longer shower than I'm allowed to and fallen gratefully into this lumpy bed. It's Saturday night, bingo night with the ladies on the mental ward, and I am a tired old broad.

With few exceptions, my evenings with the ladies are peaceful and reasonably pleasant. Tonight was one of the exceptions. For some reason the women had been edgy all afternoon. They had nagged the COs into making three calls to my floor during the day to be sure I'd be there that evening, though I always come when I say I will.

I was fifteen minutes late because a CO escort couldn't be found to walk me to West Wing. After four o'clock an inmate can't move from one building to another unless accompanied by an officer. It may make sense in winter, but it's silly in summer, when at eight o'clock it's often brighter than winter's three-thirty.

Cora met me at the door to tell me breathlessly, for the twentieth time, that her son is now in a drug program, "And doin' fine." Barbara told me Jo Jo's in lock and Mary's gone to Marcy. Charlotte asked the first inevitable question, "Do you have any cigarettes tonight?" and Jackie the inevitable second one, "Where's the Kool-Aid?" I'm not sure it's because they like the Kool-Aid so much as because they find comfort in the sameness of things, the security of knowing that what came first last week will come first again this week. We always fix the Kool-Aid first. Barbara does it all by herself now. Then Lillian passes the lollipops or the Crispy Crunchies, as they call them, which I make for them whenever I can manage to get Rice Krispies and marshmallows together at the same time. Then we spread all the bingo prizes out on the Ping-Pong table so everyone has plenty of time to smell the soap or finger whatever they think they might like to win. Finally, the game begins.

But not tonight. While we were putting out the prizes, Pinky had a seizure, grunting, shaking wildly, foaming at the mouth, spitting up, throwing her large body about. She had cracked her skull open Wednesday morning during a seizure, leaving a wide, deep gash that required stitches. The women grew frightened, and Vicky yelled, "Get her head. Get something under her head so's she don't crack it again." The women reached her first to help her while the COs ambled casually toward her. It always happens this way, whoever is having the seizure. "She's just doing it to get attention," the COs often say. You couldn't fake what Pinky was going through. I don't know what connection there is between epilepsy and crime, but Bedford seems to me to be the epilepsy center of the world. It is not unusual to see at least one seizure a day somewhere on the grounds. I believe the fact that so many of the women were smacked in the head as little children plays some role.

While everyone's attention was centered on Pinky, Tony ran out of the room, only to return two minutes later to announce, "Hey, Jean, I just vomited. Don't start yet. I gotta clean it up." She marched back and forth with mop and pail while I assured everyone to relax and not to worry. "We won't start until everyone is ready."

At five to seven we were about to begin when Cornelia announced she wanted to sing me a hymn, which she then did. I'm not sure of its name. The tune was a sad, strange crooning. Finally, the song ended, and having led Virgie back to her seat after she had tried to gather up most of the prizes into her bathrobe and take them back to her cell, the game began. Virgie has good weeks and bad weeks, mostly the latter these days. She was awarded parole many months ago, but the parole department still hasn't found a place for her to go out to except a public shelter, which is hardly the place for a partially crippled, almost-seventy-year-old mental case. In time she may grow accustomed to the idea that this could be her home forever. She isn't at peace with it now, God knows.

With the exception of Mary and Pat arguing over who called whose mother a bitch, the evening proceeded peacefully. I'm tired now that the evening is over, yet gratified, as I usually am. There is no group of women here who show their gratitude for each small thing done for them, who even take the time, if they are able, to write an occasional note of thanks, as these women do. They don't take any kindness for granted. Interesting, isn't it? We didn't start and we don't continue the program to win brownie points, but it makes these women special some-how that the phrase "thank you" plays a role in their vocabu-lary. It is a stranger, a foreigner, to so many people here.

Love,
Very Sleepy

July 10, 1990

Dear Shana,

There is presently no pharmacist at the prison. We had a good one for a while but like so many other competent staff people, he finally quit in disgust. Since then we've had a con-stant parade of new faces handing out pills, including the girl who used to run the switchboard! Prescriptions can take anywhere from three days to five weeks to be filled, this in a prison with over 850 permanent residents and another 1,500 women who pass through on their way to other prisons, a large majority of whom have some medical problem. It may be anything from AIDS, cancer, TB, high blood pressure, diabetes, seizures, gall bladder infections, syphilis, sickle cell anemia, still-uncured infections from dirty needles, paralysis, paranoia, to plain old cramps. For a while, local drugstores filled our prescriptions until, we're told, unpaid bills were so large they refused to give further service. I guess Medicaid is supposed to pay some or all of these bills, but I really don't know. Some of our women are now driven to Albany (a three-hour drive) to have standard operations and treatment that is available twenty minutes away. Right now they have a driver take our prescriptions to Fishkill Prison (an hour-and-a-half drive there and back plus a CO's time when he has to be replaced here). When will the public begin to take an honest look at prisons? What kind of a country or community looks to its prisons for growth in employment even though it is patently clear that they fail in so much of their mission? In fact, they still aren't sure what their mission is. Will I ever stop looking for logic? I'm sure it would increase my life expectancy if I did.

Jean

July 14, 1990

Dear Shana,

Lunch with Ivana and the ladies! What a treat. I hope your skirt was just as short as everyone else's. Ivana's daughter was probably just as happy that you were there as you were to find her. Having put my own children through a tragic and very public kind of hell, I feel deeply for youngsters who have to survive on the sidelines while their parents hit the tabloids. There must be some pretty wretched days in school. "Did you know your daddy was cheating on your mommy?" "Whadda ya think you'll call Marla if they get married?" "Is your mother still gonna be rich?"

I hear in your letters the same discomfort with a group of women that I have felt all my life, the feeling they all have secrets you can never know, an ongoing concern over things you really don't care about. It isn't a question of being more or less feminine; it's simply a missing ingredient in us or an extra one in them. There were moments outside when I felt quite superior because of it, and many more when I felt socially inadequate and wanting to hide. Your relief at leaving the party leaves me suspecting you've shared those feelings. Of course, there's always the chance that half the other ladies in the room felt the same way. Is it good or bad that we all hide so much?

Damn it! As I write that, I'm beginning to cry. I wonder what makes you cry, Shana. You never say. I recognize and criticize egocentrism so quickly in others, but now I see so much of it in myself—especially so in here. My letters to you are proof positive of it—what I care about, what I find interesting, what I just learned. Do you ever want to scream, "Shut up and listen to me for a while"? At least this way you don't have to write long letters in response. You know I'll write again.

Jean

July 16, 1990

Dear Shana,

I clipped out Carolyn Heilbrun's essay "Women Writers Coming of Age" and just reread it again with pleasure. My coming of age is in my sixties, but then my adolescence was delayed until my forties, so it's understandable.

She quotes Toni Morrison's character Pilate from *Song of Solomon*.

When she realized what her situation in the world was and would probably always be, she threw away every assumption she had learned and began at zero. First off she cut her hair. That was one thing she didn't want to think about anymore. Then she tackled the problem of trying to decide how she wanted to live, and what was valuable to her. When am I happy and when am I sad and what is the difference? What do I need to know to stay alive? What is true in the world? Her mind traveled crooked streets and aimless goat paths, arriving sometimes at profundity, other times at the revelations of a three-year-old.

I think I may have found a kindred soul in Pilate, with some possible caveats. When I think about it all, I still imagine the living room draperies in the cabin matching the quilted material on the couch. Does that mean I'm still just in the process of coming of age, or can I creep under the wire now? My hair is no longer a problem. I've been cutting it myself for nine years, with ragged results, but it doesn't bother me. Clothes aren't as important as they once were and probably never will be again, though occasionally I do imagine something beyond these green pants. I've saved a pattern from a box of them someone sent us. It's of a long, loose fitted dress. I intend to learn how to make it myself in many different colors, starting with orange. I think I'll have one Chanel suit, too, circa 1980, so there's enough fabric in the skirt to cover the pubic area. It could be useful if I ever leave the woods and the dog and the Connecticut River long enough to "get dressed up." All of it is on hold, of course, until I am permitted again out into the world.

I almost feel self-conscious imagining myself outside this insane tomb. I wonder if I'll be able to cross a street by myself. It's dancing right on the edge of trouble to think about myself. Better to concentrate on the ladies and the babies. I sleep better that way.

Good night, I hope

July 19, 1990

Dear Shana,

The summer has become for me the most enervating time of year, not because of the heat but because of the role I play in the Children's Center. I see the children less and less. Instead, I look a little more closely into their lives while mother is here in prison, and I shuffle paper ad nauseam, trying to arrange times mutually agreeable to mother, guardian, host family, social agency, prison facility, Children's Center funds, and facilities to bring the children into our summer program.

I feel for the mothers who have lost control over the whereabouts and well-being of their children. I want to throttle the ones who obviously never assumed that control when they were out on the street. There seems to be an increasing number of the latter, as crack has moved into mother's first concern and children fit in between the cracks. Two years ago we had 200 children in the summer program. This summer we will have approximately 150, though there are 200 more women here than there were a few years ago.

One child's guardian wrote us, "You can take the kid this week and every week for the rest of the summer." "The kid" is six years old and probably knows only too well how little he is wanted in the place he now calls home. One mother-in-law who has the children told Sister Elaine, "If there were any way I could do it, I'd serve out her time for her. She is such a wonderful mother. Her little girls adore her, and they need her." We run the gamut. There's no generalizing about mothers.

Two children will not be here because nobody knows where they are. "His father come and took him for the weekend three weekends ago and we don't know where to look. I think he's got 'em back in Puerto Rico. He don't want the kid. He's just tryin' to get back at me." The boy is nine.

"There's been bad trouble in my mother's house. The police came. My husband come and took her because it's no place for a child to be. He's got a regular job. I don't know who's taking care of her." She's six. They are only two of our Bedford children born with what Jonathan Kozol calls "the implacable inheritance of a diminished destiny."

A number of the guardians have no phone or tell the mother this so she won't call and reverse the charges. It's hard to reach them by mail. "They broke into all the mail boxes last week," and messages left with neighbors are rarely delivered. Many of the mothers speak no English and can't even read the Spanish we so carefully translate our notices into. Listening skills are not high on our list of accomplishments in here.

Some mothers who have only two children when they enter prison suddenly have five when they sign up for the summer program, hoping to place a few nieces or neighbors in the program, too. Its purpose, however, is to bring mothers and children together, not others.

We have had at least five mothers apply who have no idea where their children live and hope Sister will find them. One woman told Sister she would like to have her son in the program but "haven't seen him in twelve years."

Each time something new occurs in the life of one of the youngsters, there are more papers to shuffle, more places to change, and at least three more phone calls to be made by any staff person who is available. For me the saddest thing was a child arriving eager to see his mother, only to discover she was moved to another prison the day before and no one was notified. Ten-year-old Paul arrived this way, dressed to the nines in all new clothes, so eager to see his mother he ran all the way from the parking lot to the Visiting Room. Told that she was gone, he burst like a small balloon. "It was all for nothing," he said. "All for nothing."

Dr. Brazelton was interviewed on TV this morning. He said 18 percent of the babies born in Boston today are addicted to some form of drug. The figure is at least that high in New York. He also said, "Every child born has the right to be loved passionately by at least one person." Carbon copy to those Right to Lifers who think breathing is all that's required.

Love,
Jean

July 29, 1990

Dear Shana,

With the medicine department in a state of chaos, I was stupid enough to run out of Inderal on a Friday, which meant that the best I could hope for was to get my prescription filled by Tuesday. And I couldn't find my prescription. Like the naive child I will always be, I went down to the nurse's station and asked for one long-acting 80 mg. Inderal pill. The nurse asked "Where's your prescription?"

"I've lost it."

"You can't get a pill without a prescription."

"I know, but since I've been taking the pill every day for almost five years, there must be a record of it in my folder. And anyway, why would I ask for it if I didn't need it and I'm not supposed to have it? There are no highs or lows from Inderal. It isn't like sniffing glue or whatever."

"Well," she huffed, "you might commit suicide with it."

"With one Inderal? If that were true, why am I still alive?"

She left most grudgingly to get my folder. I was sitting on a bench when she returned and hovered over me with a look that Carol Burnett might have assumed for her role in *Little Orphan Annie*. "Well," she said, "you're *not* getting *any* Inderal!"

"You mean I'm to go without it until I can make an appointment with a doctor?"

"Exactly."

"But why?"

"According to your record, you haven't had any Inderal prescribed since last November."

"And because you nurses don't keep the records up to date, I'm to go without medication I am told must be taken daily?"

"If you were getting it when you say you were, it would be in your folder."

A week later, when I saw the doctor, he pointed to the place where he had clearly listed my prescriptions, and they were up to date.

Love,
Jean

July 30, 1990

Dear Shana,

It's late and I'm confused. I discovered something today that leaves me wondering what to do. I know what's right; I don't know what's safe, and this time my instinct is to protect me, if that's possible. For the second time in my life, I find myself the victim of egregious malpractice. At least this time I recognized it before it's much too late, and this time lives are not imperiled. It's frightening nonetheless.

They've started processing my plea for clemency again, repeating all the gestures we went through last time. I was told, "You will have to be seen by two psychiatrists to be evaluated. They will call you shortly." The psychiatrist I see every three weeks, who asks me if I have any problems and renews my prescription for 75 mg. of Tofranil, called me for a special conference yesterday. He asked me how old I am, whether I hear voices, and a few other searching questions and then assured me I had completed my evaluations for clemency. I told him I still hadn't seen a second doctor, and he said, "Oh, yes you have. You must have forgotten about Dr. Prieto." I told him I hadn't forgotten Dr. Prieto. I had literally never seen Dr. Prieto and wouldn't know him if I bumped into him. Nonetheless, Dr. Prieto has written an evaluation of me for the Clemency Board.

Who could possibly have told him to write it? Why didn't he say "I don't know the woman"?

I asked the doctor to let me see the report. He said, "I can't, but it's all good stuff, so what difference does it make if he saw you or not?" I was insistent enough so he finally showed me the report briefly. "But don't tell anyone that I showed it to you." Among other things, Prieto wrote that I should take a drug rehabilitation course as a requirement for clemency. His suggestions must spring from newspaper stories of ten years ago that disclosed that I had been prescribed Desoxyn by Dr. Tarnower for nine years, a drug known on the street as speed and which I shouldn't have been given for nine days. I have never used a drug that was not recommended and prescribed by a doctor. In prison I have used nothing but required heart medicine and progressively smaller amounts of an antidepressant. The smaller doses have been at my request, never the doctor's. Yet, though the Clemency Board never gives reasons for denial, this report could be used to keep me in prison for five more years. And I've learned of it quite by accident.

I think Prieto should be reported, but if I tell Michael,[*] and he reports it, they can always deny the whole thing. They're quite capable of it, and I will be the heavy. Prieto is now old and ill. Please don't mention this to Michael. I feel better having put it in writing to one person at least.

I often think in here of the frustration I must have been to my husband because I insisted the world was a good place and people were to be trusted. I didn't connect life to what I'd read in history books. And I'm afraid some of that quality still clings. I am genuinely shocked by what Prieto has done, and I don't think anyone else is. I should have been reading more novels all this time and planting fewer petunias.

Love,
Jean

---

[*]Michael Kennedy, one of Jean Harris's lawyers.

August 10, 1990

Dear Shana,

I'm glad you told Judge F. about Prieto. Her description of it as "psychiatric gangsterism" is apt, I think. I finally decided to write to Superintendent Lord and ask to see her. She called me to her office. I told her what had happened and said Prieto's fate was up to her, but what I wanted for me was to have his evaluation of me removed from my file, along with anything else that might have his name on it. She said she would see that that was done.

Obviously she is more worldly wise than I. She didn't seem at all surprised by anything I told her. It was a friendly conversation, and we ended by extolling the beauties of New Hampshire.

Love,
Disillusioned—something
I'm really too old to be

August 15, 1990

Dear Shana,

Happily, the media have begun to discover our neglected littlest children. Whether they will "do" babies and then go on to something that sells better time will tell. George Will wrote a column recently in *Newsweek* entitled "Mothers Who Don't Know How." "An infant," he wrote, "can fail to develop some early brain functions as a consequence of social deprivation, and that developmental loss most probably will never be made up."

René Spitz published the same information in 1946 and produced a chilling film of infants in an orphanage literally dying of loneliness for lack of love and nurturing even though their physical needs were being adequately met. He also studied and observed that infants who spent the first year of their lives in a prison nursery with their mothers showed greater intellectual and emotional growth in a year's time than did those in a well-run, humane orphanage or in a lower socioeconomic family. Having known this for fifty years, there is presently one state prison system in the United States that permits babies to spend the first year of their lives with an incarcerated mother—even if she is in a top-security prison—and that's New York State.

Anthony Lewis, in an Op-Ed column, writes: "Every year one million teenage girls get pregnant; two and one half million adolescents contract a sexually transmitted disease. More than one million are regular users of drugs. Alcohol-related accidents are the leading cause of death among teenagers."

The *New York Times* headlined on its front page "Administration Rejects Proposal for New Anti-Poverty Program." An administrative spokesman explained, "We concluded there were no obvious things we should be doing that we weren't doing that would work." Likewise, the White House acknowledged that "a major or new investment in children would have a big payoff for American society in the long run, but it shelved the idea after concluding that it was not likely to show an immediate reward." We criticize people, especially children, for wanting immediate gratification when it's a national policy.

Fondly,
Jean

August 18, 1990

Dear Shana,

On the way up the hill today a woman said to me, "My, Mrs. Harris, you sure do move along good—considering your age." There is something about being told you do something well—considering your age—that does not lift the spirits on first hearing. On second thought, it's something to be grateful for.

Another woman stopped to tell me she is petitioning to have a special housing unit for the "older ladies." I don't think there are four of them as old as I am, and even if there were, it's not a good idea. Short of being put with nothing but teenagers, I can think of nothing worse than a bunch of old ladies. I'll take a mix, thank you.

Love,
The Old Lady

August 19, 1990

Dear Shana,

Space at the kitchen window was at a premium this afternoon while we all strained our necks watching a wedding ceremony taking place at the far end of the yard. Two of the ladies were getting married. The "minister" was the bride's former lover of a few weeks ago. His/her present lover was the maid of honor. This is known as "the extended family" in prison. The groom (I'm told "spouseling" is the accepted new term), the best man, and the minister were all in tails, the tails made by cutting up state clothes to match the green slacks on two of them, a sheet or something white cut to match the white (kitchen service) pants worn by the preacher. The bride (spouselette) was in long white stockings, white shorts, white

138

blouse, and white floral arrangement in her hair. The one touch of color was two bright red marks on her neck that called out for attention and looked as though she had been making it with Dracula.

The COs as usual were slow to notice an unusual number of women gathered closely in one area. CO Davis, officer on our floor, took one look and raced downstairs to sound an alarm, her sense of propriety outraged. We're told that when she screamed at the male CO in charge of the yard to "do something," he answered, "Hell, Davis, what was I supposed to do? By the time I got there, they were throwing rice."

By the time the happy couple were "receiving," two sergeants had appeared, and four other COs. They stood around looking foolish and utterly useless until the yard's closing time, when the spouseling and spouselette had to return to their respective floors. Angela wound up the proceedings as we finally left the window with "Well, you have to give her credit. She sure didn't marry for money." "She didn't marry for looks, either," CO Davis sniffed, still furious because no one had been given a Charge Sheet.

The marriage met with disaster the next morning when the groom was transferred to another prison. In the meantime, the bride had asked to be transferred from a reasonably clean and comfortable housing unit to the back building, where there are no cells, only cubicles and double bunking, where the groom had been living. There is no way to lock anyone in, so musical beds are one of the favorite forms of amusement. No one thinks there will be a long mourning period.

I still haven't found out for sure whether it is against corrections rules to hold mock weddings—of the same sexes or opposites. You can marry a civilian while you're here even if you have a life sentence without parole—and people do. Too much fraternizing between inmates can be a real security risk because domestic quarrels, when they do break out, can be vicious. But then, if you put it in writing that people of the same sex cannot get married, you would soon have the ACLU on your back, and the whole gay community as well. We really do keep piling problems on ourselves, don't we? I wonder how colleges handle this today. When I was at Smith in 1941–45, getting married meant leaving college at once. That was changed long ago. Now can two women marry at Smith or two men at Princeton? I wonder.

Our Sunday wedding, I suspect, was less a love match than a burning desire to find one more way for the "bride and groom" to thumb their noses at the system. It pumped up the facility adrenaline for a little while, and that's worth something.

Love,
Jean—who is very grateful
she is an old woman!

August 29, 1990

Dear Shana,

With our 11th Summer Program for inmate children now behind us, parenting classes will begin again, with one large change that has evolved over the past year and a half. The class called Intensive Parenting is no more, for now at least. A new course is to take its place and be called Choices and Changes, a far better name for the curriculum Lucia has devised. The course will be built entirely around self-examination (psychological, not physical) and be taught by Lucia.

We've seen "self-esteem" become a national buzzword, too often facile and meaningless, too often and too easily promised as the prize at the end of talking, not the end of personal effort. The course will pose questions each woman must seek to answer for herself, and will endeavor to help her with the search where it can. Self-esteem will not be the subject, though each woman may be a little closer to it when the course is completed. The hope is that with a clearer picture of their own values they will be better prepared to shuck off the ego-centrism so common to deprived youth and to think with more concern about the needs of others, especially the needs of their own children. By then they may be better prepared to care about and profit from a course in parenting. It's worth a try, and Lucia is a very good teacher.

Hopefully,
Jean

September 7, 1990

Dear Shana,

In the past three weeks I've read Dostoyevski's *House of the Dead* and Gogol's *Dead Souls*, both quite by chance. The Gogol was lying somewhere in a box of used paperbacks. The Dostoyevski Laura Haywood sent me. She has sent me a book almost every week for ten years, with the result that my reading has reached new heights of eclecticism. In spite of its name, *Dead Souls* is quite amusing. It's sort of the czarist version of *Liar's Poker*. Dostoyevski's *Brothers Karamazov* is one of my five lifetime favorite books and the only novel I've read three times. This quote from *House of the Dead* struck me where I live. "A man who has once experienced power and the possibility of humiliating another creature with the deepest kind of humiliation somehow loses control over his own sensations. Tyranny is a habit; it can develop and it does develop ultimately into illness."

You can't tell the Russians much about jailers. They've had more than their share of them, before the Revolution as well as after it. I've had more than my share of a few of them now, too, especially a Sergeant X, male, and CO Endor. Sergeant X is a large, simple bully of a man whose stomach precedes him wherever he goes. My first introduction to him was a day about fifty of us were waiting in 113 Rec Room to be allowed to go to work. Someone has decided it makes more sense for us to leave for afternoon classes in two stages rather than one, so we are called from our cells to 113 Rec Room, mill around in a dirty, crowded, smoke-filled room for anywhere from five to twenty minutes, and then we go to work. The door to the room was open that day, so I stepped out into the lobby to get my breath. "Here! Get back in there," the Sergeant called. "It's just for a minute," I said. "I really can't breathe in there." "I don't care if you can breathe or not," he yelled. "Get back in there." The only thing missing was a cattle prod.

CO Endor always greets me in a high falsetto voice. "Well, here come Princess Di. Where you goin' in such a hurry, Princess Di? You ain't in no hurry. You got time. You got plenty time."

There are no straws under the fingernails in here, just daily doses of gratuitous unkindness and nastiness. They kill the spirit the way they tell me arsenic kills the body—a little bit at a time.

Love,
Princess Di

September 10, 1990

Dear Shana,

I spent this afternoon in the yard with a young woman I don't think I've ever mentioned to you. Her name is Kelly. I noticed her the first week I arrived. She had a freshness about her, short, naturally curly hair, a lovely, clear complexion, rosy cheeks, and a kind of complete innocence about her. She had come to Utica, New York, from a farm in High Point, North Carolina, looking for adventure, I suppose, fleeing from boredom, or perhaps fleeing from a small town's reaction to what was considered unforgivable there. Kelly is a lesbian. She and a young man had been tried and found guilty of a gas station robbery in which the attendant was killed. They had each been given twenty-five years to life.

The crime was committed in 1972. Immediately after it, a Mr. Hyland had come forward and said he had gotten gas at the station shortly before the crime and the young man who gave him gas was not the regular worker there. He identified Kelly's codefendant as the one who had given him gas. He said he also saw someone there in a parked car but the person had "a lot of hair" and he couldn't see the face. The car was Kelly's, which she sometimes lent him.

Almost three years after the crime, out of the blue, Kelly was arrested because she was a known friend of the man believed to have filled Mr. Hyland's gas tank. The two had met in a gay bar in Utica, and occasionally she lent him her car while she was at work. She had no police record at all. Her first arrest was at her parents' home in North Carolina. She was jailed for a short time until the judge said, "There isn't enough evidence to hold her. There's nothing here." All charges were dropped. A month and a half later, a governor's warrant was issued from New York. She was again arrested and this time held in a North Carolina jail for almost a year before she could be extradited to New York. It was almost another year before her case came to trial. The district attorney offered to drop the murder charge against her if she would plead guilty to robbery. She refused and went to trial.

After being shown pictures of Kelly and pressured by publicity and the eagerness of the police to solve the crime, Mr. Hyland, three years after signing an affidavit that he did not see the face of the person in the car, suddenly changed his mind and in court identified Kelly as the other person he had seen at the gas station. He had even sworn he didn't know whether the person was a man or a woman. Based on his courtroom identification alone, Kelly was sent to prison for twenty-five years.

When I first met Kelly, her codefendant had just signed a sworn statement that she was not at the gas station and had had absolutely nothing to do with the crime. He still claims it. He didn't swear it during the trial, since he had pled innocent. To exonerate her would have been to incriminate himself. Unfortunately, judges give little or no credence to such ex post facto statements. Their attitude, understandably in some cases, is "He has nothing to lose now. What the hell."

In court Kelly was represented by a young man whose field is corporate law and who had never before tried a criminal case. Several years later, Claudio Angelo, a professor of law at New York University, with the help of some of his students, began to work on her case. In 1985, after she had served twelve years, the U.S. Circuit Court of the Southern District of New York granted her a writ of habeas corpus, Judge David Edelstein presiding. Kelly's application was based on whether the court identification of her was unconstitutionally tainted. The magistrate found that it was and ordered the court to release her or give her a new trial. The decision states: "The court finds that the pretrial occurrences were unduly suggestive. . . . Further, the court agrees with the magistrate that there was no independent and reliable basis for in-court identification by Hyland."

Kelly was offered the opportunity to plea-bargain and have her sentence reduced to fifteen to life or have a new trial. Against the urging of most of her probably wiser friends in prison, she refused to take the plea. "I didn't commit a crime. I never have nor would I rob a person or kill them, and I don't want to go through the rest of my life as a convicted felon."

She would be out of prison by now if she had taken the plea. I don't believe any guilty person after twelve years of incarceration would have turned down that plea.

The district attorney, not wanting to give her another trial, appealed the district court's decision up to the circuit court and won. It did not say the magistrate's decision was wrong per se but that since Kelly's young lawyer had not made an issue of the constitutionality of the way the identification was made in the first court, he didn't have the right to bring it up on appeal.

Following this grim setback, Sister Clair, a friend, and a young lawyer went to see Mr. Hyland to persuade him to stand by his first sworn statement. In the course of a long, rather self-pitying conversation, he complained about the position he was in, the pressures that have been put on him over the years. "They heckled me at home. They heckled me at work." He gave them the impression he might sign a statement that he had been wrong, or at least not certain, in his courtroom identification. Unfortunately, they didn't hand him a pen and paper on the spot, and now he says he will stick to his statement made in court contradicting the statement he signed several days after the crime, eighteen years ago.

By the time Kelly has spent twenty-five years here, the taxpayers will have spent almost $1 million to punish her. If justice doesn't move them, you'd think economics would. Don't ever be sanguine about justice, Shana. Who the hell can say what it is.

Jean

September 19, 1990

Dear Shana,

Did I tell you about Johnnie? She's a woman I met here years ago. She was in the process of a series of operations that would change her from a man to a woman. She had been sent first to Sing Sing, apparently had serious problems there, and then was sent here. She didn't have a much better reception here. She was still ambivalent, both physically and emotionally, as to what she was. She became something of an exhibitionist; some of the women didn't like it and complained, so the state decided that Sing Sing was, after all, the place for her, and she was sent back. I can remember clearly standing in 114 yard with her one day, while she complained about where the state should put her, and asking her, "Johnnie, if you aren't sure yourself where they should put you, how is the state supposed to know?"

Today she is a beaming, attractive female brunette. She came through Bedford recently on a charge she assured me was "nothing really. I'll be going right out." She called to me in the clinic, "Hey, Jean, remember me? I'm Johnnie. Did ya read about me in the papers? I won my case against the state. They gave me sixty-five thousand dollars for putting me in Sing Sing when I should have been at Bedford." In today's world, every infant layette should include the telephone number and a letter of introduction to a good lawyer. That's half the battle right there.

Love,
Jean

September 25, 1990

Dear Shana,

People often ask me why I don't write a novel. Come to think of it, why don't you? You could do it. I can't. I am merely an observer, a listener, a reporter. I can rarely talk myself into reading a novel, even though I usually enjoy the few I read. The most recent one was Jeanette Hain's *All of It*. I found it quite lovely, with the added attraction that it's short. Do you know her?

I heard Bill Moyers interview her. Some of their highly intellectual conversation about music was way over my head, but part of it I think I understood. She told how the precise, required structure in great music, which she has spent a lifetime studying, must be carried over into great writing. "The best art, the best thinking, is always highly structured," she said.

I'm sure she's right, which is most depressing. I've reached a stage in my thinking where everything seems connected, where I'm convinced everything *is* connected, so one thing leads easily to another, and what I once might have labeled as rambling now seems like logical, even organized thinking. I'm afraid the point of all that logic is more and more lost on others. Could the problem possibly be with me?

Love,
Puzzled, as always

September 28, 1990

Dear Shana,

You sounded so low when we spoke this morning I thought I'd send you a small treasure to cheer you. You will be the first girl on your block to have one.

I don't know if I mentioned to you that for the past year this "correctional facility" has been going through a very expensive process called "accreditation." This has involved painting everything you can't put in storage, fixing sinks that have been broken for the past three to five years, adding another layer of razored fencing, and building a new $1 million front entrance, complete with a gun tower. This place needs a gun tower like the COs need lobotomies, but a gun tower is required for a top-security prison that aspires to accreditation. The tower is carefully located so that, standing in its topmost corner, you couldn't shoot an escaping inmate in any of the logical escape areas, but it's just right for taking potshots at cars and any friendly neighbors who happen to be passing by.

At any rate, the good news is out, and Bedford is now an "accredited" prison. The Superintendent was moved to tears by the good news, but apparently not too surprised, since she had had the foresight to have pins made for all of us. And now you can wear one of them. As you see, the pin reads, "I'm from Bedford and proud of it." Tell me you can sport that on your bosom and feel blue.

What more can I say to cheer you?

Love,
Jean

October 1, 1990

Dear Shana,

The biggest news this morning is that seventy-one heads of state, more than have ever met together before in all of history, have gathered here in New York City to do good for little children. One thing is for sure: Everyone wants to be counted; everyone wants to pat at least one little head.

They have signed a Declaration on Children, a lengthy document starting with a litany on the condition of children in the world today, a list to make all of us hang our heads in shame, and a still longer section listing all the goods and services that they plan to make available to children all over the world, someday. The plan they endorse will "drastically improve the lives of children." Since 14 million children presently die worldwide before they reach the age of five, "drastic improvement" is in order.

"The children of the world are innocent, vulnerable, and dependent. They are also curious, active, and full of hope. Their time should be one of joy, peace, of playing, learning, and growing. Their future should be shaped in harmony and cooperation. Their lives should mature as they broaden their perspectives and gain new experience." I can only suppose this is a quick translation from another language. Whatever it is, it's a sure winner of the Nobel and Pulitzer prizes for hypocrisy. They could have added that within ten years every child in the world under five shall have a big teddy bear from Bloomingdale's. An extra $20 billion is needed within the decade to make those good things happen. So far there are nickels and dimes in the hat.

Each of the seventy-one heads of state was permitted to make a short, timed speech. Many took the occasion to say that sooner or later raising living standards of Third World children may depend on limiting population growth. The declaration itself states: "Emphasis must be placed on responsible planning, on family size, and on children spacing. The family, as a fundamental group and natural environment for the growth and well-being of children, should be given all necessary protection and assistance." Did President Bush sign this? How could he? It certainly isn't what he preaches in his own country. He could afford his five children. Others, like Toni, one of the children in our summer program this year who is pregnant with twins at the age of thirteen, can't. Her president says to have an abortion is murder, never mind the cost in tragedy for her and her children and the cost in dollars for everyone. Figure about a quarter of a million dollars for incubators for the two babies and heaven knows what other hospital expenses, then welfare or, more expensive, foster care, which we all know is a disaster. How could Bush sign anything that pledges family planning and child spacing? Toni came to the summer program and cried when Sister Elaine wouldn't let her go to the gym to play with the other kids. It was the first time that she seemed to be aware that being six months' pregnant with twins made her different from the other thirteen-year-old kids.

Our congressmen have now taken five months to not arrive at an annual budget. We wrapped up the problems of our kids over a short weekend. Is it possible I have become a cynic?

Jean

October 3, 1990

Dear Shana,

Of all the things in this world that puzzle and confound me, I think anti-Semitism comes somewhere near the top of the list. I have never understood it, and it never seems to go away.

Like my mother and quite unlike my father, I always judged people from the neck up and simply took on faith that their hearts were good, too. That ultimately led to disaster for me, but I could have learned that particular lesson from an Episcopalian, too, so it hasn't changed in any way my feeling for many friends who happen to be Jews.

In 1944, when I was a junior at college, I wrote a paper on "The Problems of the Jews," not "The Jewish Problem." For almost two years I had clipped articles from the papers about what was happening to Jews in Europe and whether or not there should be an Israel. When anyone tells you today, "We didn't know," it's pure garbage. It was all there on the front page of the paper week after week. I can't say I was appropriately overwhelmed by the immensity of the evil of it. It was too awful to fully comprehend.

We've now spent forty-five years saying, "Remember, it was those rotten Germans who did it, not us. . . . We'd have done something if only we'd known." And we make TV specials about the Holocaust to cleanse our souls or make a buck, not necessarily in that order.

Perhaps because I can only concentrate on one aspect of the downfall of man at a time, I went through years of tucking the Jewish problem away in the solved-better-than-other-problems department, even though I'm only too aware that the Grosse Pointes and Bronxvilles of our world will probably never learn.

Tonight I settled into bed with the *New York Times*, and there was still another article on the burgeoning anti-Semitism that is once again boiling to the surface. In the last few months I've seen articles about it in Russia, Hungary, Poland, New York City, the University of Michigan, Madison, Wisconsin, and now Dartmouth College, more specifically in the *Dartmouth Review*, a very, very politically conservative student weekly newspaper, though what conservatism has to do with anti-Semitism, I don't know. Just before the start of Yom Kippur the *Review* ran this quotation from Adolf Hitler's *Mein Kampf*: "I believe today that I am acting in the sense of the Almighty Creator. By warding off the Jews I am fighting for the Lord's work."

That Christ was crucified by the Jews can't be the reason for anti-Semitism today. The people who preach it can't be considered Christians. I wonder what they can be considered.

I've read a lot in the past twenty years about learned and

innate behavior. We've been gradually moving things from the learned to the innate column, notably the skills that help us to handle language. I've about decided the need for scapegoats is innate, too. The more aware we are of the world's tragedies, and heaven knows we've never been as aware of them as we are now, and the more aware we are of our own limitations and failures, the more we need the solace of pointing the finger of blame away from ourselves. The trouble with Jews is they keep rising phoenixlike from their own ashes instead of settling into slums and crying, "It's everyone else's fault that I'm no damn good." This is a very aggravating quality, and obviously hard to forgive. We're afraid to tell some people to "shape up," but we aren't afraid to tell Jews, "We dislike you for shaping up."

I know along the road you've experienced your share of anti-Semitism. It is an ugly, hateful, beastly thing. I would be deeply sorry to think any of it came your way from someone thinking she was befriending me by hating Jews.

Love,
Jean

October 8, 1990

Dear Shana,

The two books I have had published have given birth to the myth in here that I know all the right people and can help other people get books published, too. I've never seen enough completed work to send to an agent or editor, not even a skeleton outline, but I've heard many say, "I'm writing a book, Jean. My life will make a great book and a great movie. You wouldn't believe what my life's been like." They're probably right. One woman did read me the opening sentence to her autobiography: "Motherhood is the second-oldest profession in the world." I told her I thought it had already been used, but she decided to go with it anyway.

I was tempted to write a book about one of the women here myself. Did you know that the last Queen of Iraq was a prisoner here for a while? At first I wasn't sure the story was true, but she lived in Sister Elaine's Providence House for a while after she was paroled, and one night after the other women in the house had derided her and her story of lost glamour and glitter, she went up to her room and brought down three large scrapbooks. "They're everything I have left," she said. For more than two hours she regaled them with pictures and newspaper clippings showing her at home with the king in the grandeur of a palace, dressed like a queen from every angle. Her royal episode was short-lived and ended the day her husband, the king, was assassinated before her eyes, and she fled for her life. I'm surprised no one has made a Monday night movie out of it. Maybe they have and I missed it.

Coreene is the most recent author to approach me for assistance. "Hey, Jean, do ya know any Japanese publishers? I've written a book in Japanese. I figure it'll get more attention that way. Anyone can write in English." I told her I didn't know any Japanese publishers and expressed surprise that she knew how to write in Japanese. "Oh, I don't know Japanese," she said. "I just write like it." She showed me a thick spiral notebook she had almost filled with page after page of figures, or characters, or designs, whatever one might call them, carefully, neatly, painstakingly drawn. I told her it looked very nice, and some of it might even look like an occasional Japanese character, but the important thing was her story. "Tell me about the story." "Oh." She shrugged. "It's not finished yet. I still got more pages to fill."

There may be a good many books better off transcribed into Coreene's Japanese. I'm sure Alfred Knopf would have agreed. Often over those pleasant Sunday lunches we enjoyed together with Helen and Hy he would give passionate sermons about the amount of trash one finds in reputable bookstores. He said there should be a special Pulitzer Prize for the publishing house that turns down the most manuscripts.

Gives a writer a slight chill and a pause for thought, don't it?

Jean

October 12, 1990

Dear Shana,

Have you heard and seen the latest political plugs for Cuomo's bid for reelection? He is actually advertising that he has built more prisons than any governor in history. This to win votes. I find it bizarre to take pride in the spending of over $1 billion from the public treasury on prisons when so far nothing has touched the problems of crime. Justice prostituted at the voting booth is a frightening thing to see. It turns me cold and leaves me with little hope for the future.

Jean

October 15, 1990

Dear Shana,

There's a woman named Karen in my class. She says she's twenty-one but she could ride half fare on the train without an argument. She has a little girl, three; a son, one and a half; and she just had another little girl two months ago. Like most

154

of the women coming here today she's here on a drug charge with a sentence of three to five.

Her questions in class, or in the few minutes at the end of class before she is hurried back to her housing unit, tell me she feels helpless and frightened about how to survive when she leaves here. "Do you think I should go back and live with my aunt when I get out of here? I wanna get away from my old friends, but she's all the family I got. Maybe I'll go to Buffalo. Whatta you think, Jean? Do you like Buffalo? I don't know anyone there. I could start over again fresh."

Today we were talking about the difference between punishment and discipline, and suddenly she said, "Jean, I was raised up by my aunt. She was good to me. She did everything she could for me. So if she was good to me, how come I'm here?" I hear that question in various disguises quite often. "Tell me, why am I bad?" "You aren't bad," I tell them. "You've made bad decisions, and now you have to learn to weigh the consequences of your actions, on yourself, on your children, on society." I say it, but the truth is, making bad decisions is what the law calls being bad. One of the women came to me yesterday and asked, "Jean, how come you call us human animals? You done it twice yesterday. I wouldn't expect you to do it. The police always call us that. 'Get in there, you animals,' they say. How come you do it, too?" I try to explain that I use it in the sense that we are among God's creatures, and the term separates us from plants. I most certainly never mean it as something rude or insulting. Another woman standing nearby assures her nothing unkind is meant. But she's still not completely sure.

These are fragile people. Ignorance leaves them very breakable. They need hours and hours and hours of a good trained, caring listener and adviser. They also need a place to live, a job, money to live on while they raise their babies, a decent friend, and just about anything else you can think of to make life bearable. I'm not a psychologist or a seer. Who am I to say why Karen is here, why she did bad things? What do I know about Buffalo? Lots of snow in Buffalo.

Jean

October 20, 1990

Dear Shana

I've been reading the short stories of Eudora Welty, one a night, the day's dessert. You can't even envy the woman. You can only stand in awe.

Love,
Jean

October 27, 1990

Dear Shana,

I have finally found my place in the pecking order of the literary world. I am an "itinerant note taker." The expression is William Buckley's, spoken on *Firing Line* this morning with that degree of hauteur and disdain he usually saves for Sister Boom Boom and Ted Kennedy. He was talking with Tom Wolfe about his recent essay in *Harper's* on the sorry state of novels in American literature today—not enough Dickenses and Tolstoys around. Apparently the piece has raised a lot of hackles, and he has become a favorite candidate for talk shows, the umpteenth time around.

The Wolfe-Buckley discussion was milder than the usual Buckley fare. They sort of circled the ring cautiously, with few crippling blows landed. Mr. B. seemed bent on finding out

156

what the theme of *Bonfire of the Vanities* is meant to be, and Mr. W. seemed just as insistent that it really didn't have one and didn't need one. I would have said its theme was clear, but then, what do I know? Buckley kept chewing away on the subject and finally said, "Well, I accept the fact that it hasn't a theme, but I feel I have to know what the theme would have been if it had had one," or words to that effect.

The seriousness with which these two bright men take themselves is part of the amusement. I do listen to Buckley whenever I can because he is a virtuoso with words and phrases, but he delivers them a little like the Lord of the Village tossing coins to the peasants, and you have to scramble for what you can get.

I have heard him be extremely learned, extremely clever, extremely cruel, and extremely funny. I don't remember hearing him be kind, but I guess that's rather a wimpish observation. I'm sure a five-minute conversation with him would leave me feeling like a spot on the carpet. The term "itinerant note taker" came out as he listed his idea of the various levels of writers. You hit rock bottom with "itinerant note taker," but I don't find it offensive for me. It's an accurate description of what I often am in here. I like the word "itinerant." It reminds me of Johnny Appleseed.

The simple sum of it is, I write because there's no one to talk with, except you, my friend, so I keep tossing apple seeds your way, and you are kind. It's a definite character flaw, you understand, but I forgive you.

Love,
Jean

November 5, 1990

Dear Shana,

Have you noticed that calling people "asshole" seems to be very popular these days? In here, of course, it's practically a term of endearment, but I read it today in good magazines, in articles by fine writers. Is it slippage on the part of writers and readers alike, or are there so many more people around who fit the description? My hunch is it's a combination of both.

What did we used to call them? As I recall, H. L. Mencken labeled them the "booboisie." I certainly never saw the word "asshole" in any of his books, though he had pretty strong feelings about the general intelligence of many people abroad in the land. "Booboisie" would hardly satisfy anyone with strong convictions on the subject today. It has too many syllables. The thought, with all the necessary disdain, requires two syllables. One isn't enough. Three are too many.

I wish I were a Mencken who could make up her own vocabulary for those times when something special seems to be in order. My mother would say of "asshole": "Nobody has to use language like that. Only ignorant people who lack words would use it." I agreed for years, but today I might give Mom an argument. There are people in here in inmate green and officer blue who fit the description so perfectly it would seem to be an injustice to designate them as anything less. I blush to tell you the word crosses my mind not infrequently these days. Sooner or later the sound will out. Imagine. A nice old lady like me.

I don't tell my sons. They wouldn't like to hear it. They would consider it a crack in my armor. Sister objects because it's unkind—to asses, which are gentle, harmless creatures. But it's too late to worry about that. Look what we did to "gay." Sorry, one and all, I don't feel apologetic. Say what you will,

Mom, my life being what it presently is, I've begun to find the word appropriate. Well, maybe not appropriate but at least satisfying when a modicum of satisfaction seems little enough to ask. I wonder what William Buckley uses when all else fails.

Love,
~ Jean

November 10, 1990

Dear Shana,

It amuses and saddens me to read all the earnest talk about teaching the young how to think when thinking is the last thing politicians look for in the American voter. If we were a nation of thinkers, if we recognized verbal garbage for what it is, if we questioned the absence of logic in much that our chosen leaders say and do, our communal and private lives as well might be quite different. Only might, mind you. We can think ourselves into corners as well as walk blindfolded into them.

Love,
Jean

November 18, 1990

Dear Shana,

"Thinkspeak" is alive and well in this prison. The truth no longer has any relationship to reality. It is whatever people in authority say. The newest memo is a monument to that brave new world. Good is bad, up is down, short is tall, cruel is kind, and damn the cheeky person who says it isn't so. Damn me!

The Package Room, which is probably the most important room in the facility, especially as the holidays approach, is in total chaos. Packages that until now have been opened in front of the inmate to whom they are addressed so she knows exactly what is in them are now opened down at the gate by a CO she will probably never see and handed to her by another CO who can easily pass the buck if something is missing. The CO at the front gate removes everything from its original packaging and dumps it into a paper bag. Any note or card that was in the package is put in an envelope and sent to the mail room, so when the inmates receive the contents of the package, they have no idea from whom it came. The card comes a day or so later through the mail. The person who hands the bag to the inmate has a pat answer if anything is missing. "Don't tell me about it. I don't open it. I'm just givin' ya what they give me."

The Sergeant who is presently in charge of the Package Room, who will tell you with all due humility, "I'm an expert in Package Room procedures," has also instituted the new requirement that if you can't have something that's sent to you, you must then and there sign a disbursement sheet to have the package mailed back. Never mind that your mother is coming tomorrow and can take it home for you. "No more packages can go out with visitors. Everything must be mailed out." The Sergeant assured me this was an improvement over simply giving things to family to take out and would be less demanding on staff. It will take a full-time person to find boxes and do all the wrapping and a full-time person in inmate accounts to handle all the disbursements that will inevitably bounce. "Are you going to garnishee their seventy-cents-a-day stipends until all the postage is paid?" I asked him. Never did get an answer. This disbursement bit has not yet been approved by administration, but most of the women, especially the new and penniless ones, don't know it, so he has them filling out disbursements he has no right to ask for. Tonight the same Sergeant came up on the floor with some lettuce, tomatoes, and cucumbers he had taken from the prison kitchen to replace some inmate food that had been taken at the front gate by parties unknown. Didn't want too many complaints during his tour. If enough disappears at the front gate and is replaced by the prison kitchen, sooner or later, one would hope, someone will complain.

A new memo for November 15, 1990, reads:"It would appear that processing (of packages) is proceeding more and more smoothly as we get used to the new system. The new system also enhances accountability on everyone's part." It virtually eliminates accountability. By doubling, even tripling, the number of COs handling inmate property, by not allowing the inmate to watch the package be opened or repackaged, by permitting weeks, even months, to go by between when the inmate turns over her property and her family receives it, there is more opportunity than ever before for theft. But what the hell. We're not talkin' about people. We're talkin' about inmates. What wretched little worlds we create and call them *correctional facilities*.

It's time to go home, Shana.

Love,
Jean

November 21, 1990

Dear Shana,

It troubles me to know that I'm responsible directly or indirectly for your receiving such a gratuitously ugly letter. For me to protest any further would only prolong the agony and cause an unwelcome proliferation of letters. Celia is an old and frail woman, not overly bright, with a streak of good intentions sandwiched in between serious blind spots and a deep sense of inadequacy.

It's the latter that produces some of our best bigots. When you introduce yourself to someone, as she did to me, with "I'm a seventh-generation Congregationalist," you can be quickly suspicious of what will follow. When she finds it necessary to apologize for being brought up in St. Louis, "a Catholic city, only because father's business took us there," you know she's impartial in her bigotry. When she assures you, "Mother was a grand sport. She had many Catholic friends, even brought 'em to the house," you know it's late in the day to start teaching her the old saw about "Do unto others as you would have them do unto you."

My father was about as loving of his fellow man as Celia, though she might be shocked to hear that at the top of Dad's hate list were Yale men, "those little pipsqueaks from Yale." His formal education, until World War I took him to Annapolis, was at Baltimore Polytechnic High School. A lot of people have to hate something or someone to plug up the hole a sense of inadequacy leaves.

I personally don't remember ever experiencing a feeling of utter contempt for another person until I came here and was treated more like a thing than a person. Now I often look at a guard and think, I wouldn't hire that little creep to empty the wastebaskets, and things far worse than that as well. Celia's letters to me are filled with childlike tales of people who have been unkind to her. She seems to have made a life's work of annoying people while thinking she is, or wanting to be, helpful. "I tried to tell the senator, but he just walked away." "She says she can't be bothered answering my calls anymore. She said I'd have to make an appointment to see her."

I don't know why I'm being so philosophical about something that is evil no matter how you try to explain it away. One person at a time, it just seems ignorant or unkind. A million people at a time, it's like the end of the world. I would have said without a thread of uncertainty in 1945 that anti-Semitism could never breed again, which just goes to show what a poor sense of history I had after all my splendid education. Today I think a sense of history comes from a good deal of living, not a good deal of reading. At this point in my life, experience tells me bigotry will disappear when, like the dinosaurs, we are wiped out by a friendly comet that comes too close. And then the rats and the cockroaches will probably start the whole thing all over again.

So you see, Virginia, there is a Santa Claus, but there's also a whole bunch of other stuff that isn't as good.

Love,
Jean

November 23, 1990

Dear Shana,

Another memo. There is to be no more hair coloring at Bedford—no dying, no streaking, no tinting. The stated reason: "Women are not to significantly change their appearance." Since a great many women come in here with dyed hair, the lack of dye will "significantly change their appearance." Ah, the joys of old age. That's one hassle I can bypass.

But these are pretty imaginative women. If it should serve

163

the purpose or the whim of a particular woman to significantly change her appearance, you can be damn sure she'll find a way. They've already discovered that the lye in the state soap can do interesting things to the hair—including make it all fall out. Ink, Kool-Aid, beet juice, and Clorox are suddenly hot-ticket items, too. She can still shave her head, or shave both sides, with a brush down the middle. Some do it just to say, "Screw you," to the world or because they lack all respect for themselves. Most of the women make a concerted effort to look nice. Their bodies are about all they have, and they work hard to keep the outside at least looking good. I do the same thing, but it ain't easy.

Love,
Jeannie with the unaltered light gray hair

November 24, 1990

Dear Shana,

We watched *Driving Miss Daisy* on the VCR tonight, and everyone loved it. When the lights came on, the woman sitting in front of me turned, stared for a moment, and said, "You sho' do favor Miss Daisy, Jean. You really do favor Miss Daisy." Miss Daisy was eighty when the lights came on. I'm being a good sport. I didn't even cry.

Love,
Methuselah

December 1, 1990

Dear Shana,

I heard Joseph Campbell remark that there is an old Polynesian saying, "He is riding on a whale, fishing for minnows." I can't get it out of my mind. It is a perfect description of America's policies toward crime. This prison is a basket full of minnows, so easily caught by their sheer numbers, only to be dumped in time back into the mainstream much as they were when they were caught.

I don't imagine the whale as representing crime per se. I think of it as the unmet potential of all of our children, for that, I'm sure, is the womb of crime.

> Jean—busily mixing her metaphors

December 5, 1990

Dear Shana,

Today the subject in parenting class was intelligence—what we mean by it, how we can help a child's intelligence to develop. As usual before class I had written the subject word on the board, and below it other words that might be useful in our discussion.

We started by seeing if the class could pinpoint what we mean when we say someone is intelligent. A person who is intelligent, they said, "talks real good," "talks real nice," "is smart," "is bright," "gets all A's," "knows a lot." And finally, because I obviously was hoping for more, one said, "We give up. Tell us."

The main purpose of this particular class was to help the mothers begin to understand that a child's development in different areas of knowing happens over a period of time, not all at once, not just because the child has begun to talk. Concepts of time, space, numbers, truth, parts and whole, and many others take time to acquire. Many little children are labeled stupid or even dishonest because what seems obvious and simple to us requires a degree of reasoning and logic their brains haven't developed yet.

I told them some of the stories Piaget told children at different ages, the questions he asked about them, and the answers he came to expect, depending upon the child's age. I was dismayed when in a few cases the answer that is usually obvious to a child of six caused argument in the class. I waited for them to work it out on their own, which they did. We talked about all the ways we could think of to help a child's reasoning powers, even a very young child's.

When class was over and I was gathering up things preparing to go back to my cell for the noon count, Virginia stopped at the door and waited for me. As we left the building she said to me quietly, "Jean, intelligence has two *l*'s in it. You had it on the board with one."

God does have his ways, doesn't he?

Luv,
Jean

December 7, 1990

Dear Shana,

You're going to a dinner dance? How awful! People over sixty shouldn't give dinner dances unless they have at least twelve living male kin to parcel out to all the widows on the guest list. People over sixty should give book-review parties or mah-jongg parties or let's-all-go-to-a-good-movie parties.

I can think of nothing less enticing than a dinner dance. (Another plus for prison. You are not invited to dinner dances.)

You sound as enthusiastic about going to one as I do, but I admire your spunk and the spirit in which you have accepted the invitation. You tell me what treasure of the opposite sex they will unearth for you is still a mystery, which adds a modicum of suspense and fun to the whole miserable experience. I can only wish you *bonne chance*, happy dancing, a safe trip home, and better you than me.

Best,
Jean

December 10, 1990

Dear Shana,

It's good news that you're going to teach a course in advanced journalism to graduate students at USC. Sooner or later everyone with a well-honed skill should teach, and heaven knows you have that skill. I know I've never thanked you enough for the number of times you've used it in my behalf, but grateful I am beyond words.

It may be difficult at first while you and the class get to know one another and they discover all the warmth and humor in the woman as well as the skill of the teacher. I'm sure you'll find disillusion there, too, if you arrive with the popular adult misconception that the young should be better than we are. But in time you'll find a few who really give a damn about something—their family, the ozone, whether the birds flew south this year—or you'll find one who doesn't give a damn about anything but has a beautiful way of saying it, and those will challenge you and make you glad you're there.

It has taken years of dealing with the law and the corrections system for me to appreciate fully the importance of being able to express oneself clearly and unambiguously and to see the tragic/comic results when we can't. Prison, this prison at least, is a place where the art of communication reaches a new low. You can get more information from a grunt, a raised eyebrow, or a screamed obscenity than you can searching for a reasoned, well-considered sentence. Writing style here has all the clarity and verve and humor of a bowl of cold oatmeal. We live in a sea of verbal mush.

I can think of nothing more important than teaching the young to think clearly and then express the thought so there is no question as to its meaning. With that daunting thought I leave the future of the Western world in your capable hands.

Be brave,
Jean

December 14, 1990

Dear Shana,

Last night Kackie's seventeen-year-old son was murdered. This morning someone called the prison to report it. The Watch Commander got the message and phoned it to the CO on Kackie's housing unit. The Watch Commander is which-ever designated person is in charge of the prison at a given moment. Ordinarily that person is the Superintendent, but in her absence it can be a number of other officers.

The CO yelled down the hall, "Hey, Kackie." Another CO said, "Don't yell like that. It's Saturday and a lot of women are sleeping." "I gotta tell her there's been a death in her family." "You mean you're gonna yell it down the hall to her?" "No. I was just gonna tell her to come up here and I'd tell her."

The other officer was decent enough to get up out of her chair and walk down the hall to tell her. This is not normal procedure, I'm told. The Watch Commander is supposed to contact the priest or minister and have him or her tell the inmate of a death in the immediate family, but it doesn't always work that way. If your child dies on a Saturday morning, it is not unusual for the person making the sad call to be told, "Call back on Monday. We can't give messages on the week-end." I know of two such cases.

As for Kackie, the news of her son's death leaves her distraught. Within the past six months her father has died of cancer, her two brothers have been killed, and her young daughter, who spent a week with her in our Summer Program, has been raped. If Kackie's lucky, and this is as lucky as she can get, she will be allowed to go to her son's funeral with a CO who will treat her with a little compassion and respect in front of what's left of her family instead of humiliating her. On the other hand, she is probably beyond feeling anything as simple as humiliation.

If anyone wonders what the drug trade does to families and the individuals in those families they could find a hundred answers in here.

Love,
Jean

December 17, 1990

Dear Shana,

Michael forwarded a letter to me today from a member of the media who asked to interview me for some program. Unfortunately, I took the time to read it, and now I've worked myself into such a state of umbrage I can't go to sleep. Hence, what follows is a How-To letter. How to write and ask Jean Harris to give an interview and be absolutely sure she won't give it.

1. Address her as "Miss Harris," the safe assumption being that since she is in prison her children are probably illegitimate.

2. Assume that she has changed drastically for the better during her incarceration and is now "rehabilitated."

3. Use several paragraphs to tell how you saved two men from death row by your interviewing prowess, and add that one of the men saved is now studying Latin and Greek.

4. Level with her and tell her you can't guarantee such dramatic results for her, but assure her she has nothing to lose.

5. Flatter her by saying, "From all that I've heard you have changed only for the best, indeed, you may have become an entirely different person."

It drives me right around the bend that anyone could presume that ten years in a public wastebasket would leave anyone better for the experience. I don't even like it when you tell me I've changed, though of course I have. Tragedy and remorse change one; learning new things changes one; one's health changes one, and growing older changes one. But prison does not make people better. Parole officers love to hear that it does, but on the whole it doesn't.

The values I've lived my whole life by are still my values. They have seen me thus far through this nightmare. The nightmare itself has done its damndest to destroy me. It has certainly added some rough verbal edges. One thing I know, Shana. I'm stronger than I've ever been before. If that's improvement, so be it.

Jean

January 1, 1991

Dear Shana,

There's this to be said for New Year's Day in prison. You never wake up with a hangover. The ladies stayed up until midnight wishing everyone a noisy and happy New Year, all of which I found singularly unjolly, so I waved a merry exit about eight o'clock and locked in to read awhile and ponder the fate of the universe.

Maybe it happens to everyone, but I find it ironic that as my own future grows shorter the things that matter most to me stretch well into the future and my personal views have become worldviews. I've been reading Betsy Griffith's fine book about Elizabeth Cady Stanton. Stanton observed that as a woman grows older she gradually finds the love she once spent on her own children reaching out to everyone's children. I've reached that state. I have never in my life felt so much caring, so much deep concern for children, even though caring about them has been my lifetime work. How to translate the caring from hand-wringing to useful action is a definite challenge in here. I guess it's a challenge anywhere.

Happy New Year, Shana, and an interesting new year for us both.

Fondly,
Jean

January 5, 1991

Dear Shana,

I watched another production of Thornton Wilder's *Our Town* this week. Strange the fascination for us that play continues to have. We line up again and again to see revivals of it

171

on the professional stage, and I'll bet I've seen ten high school performances, often as good as anything Broadway produces. There's a degree of innocence required that one can still find remnants of in high school but which can only be portrayed on Broadway.

I guess we cling to it because we enjoy all that nostalgia for a time when life was simpler and we think we were nicer. Or we like to pretend it's the way we still are under all the veneer of our new world. Sadly, the people who lived it are dead or in the process of dying. My grandmother was one of them. My mother almost was. I lived a little piece of it during the thirties. But it can't be today and yesterday, too, though I think there's enough hubris around to suppose we can arrange it. The myth of Adam and Eve becomes more meaningful to me daily. The constant temptation to take another step and still try to see things from where we were last standing is a fool's errand. We're long since east of Eden.

Love,
Jean

January 8, 1991

Dear Shana,

I'm told there's a new study coming out soon indicating that 80 percent of the children of inmates end up with a prison record. I find that hard to believe. If it's true, then God and everybody else should be ashamed. God if it's biological, the rest of us if it isn't.

I've just finished reading Jerome Bruner's little book *Acts Of Meaning*. I can't say I understood all of it but what I did understand certainly expresses a different point of view from Stanton

Samenow's. Bruner writes, ". . . it is culture and the search for meaning that is the shaping hand, biology that is the constraint, and . . . culture even has it in its power to loosen that constraint." He does add, though, "For all its generative inventiveness human culture is not necessarily benign, nor is it noticeably malleable in response to troubles. It is still customary . . . to lay the blame for the failings of human culture on human nature whether as instincts, original sin or whatever."

With little to go on but instinct and hope, I'm with Bruner. Stanton leaves you stuck with the notion that poor people have rotten kids and rich people have good ones, otherwise why are so many poor and so few rich in prison? Is prison the final settling basin where human sediment comes to rest? I can't look at the beautiful little babies in this prison nursery and believe they're doomed from birth, because of the arrangement of their DNA, to end up in prison—whatever the tests about identical twins may have shown. I can't believe that a loving parent and a healthy environment could not save them, assuming they weren't hopelessly damaged by the time they were born. Can nature and nurture ever be completely separated, so many percentage points for one, so many percentage points for the other? I don't think so.

Love,
Jean

January 11, 1991

Dear Shana,

By now you know that New Year's Eve rolled around, and with it rolled around the Governor's third denial of clemency, for me or anyone else. The letter from the Clemency Bureau arrived today, and it reads: "It has been determined that there is insufficient basis to warrant the exercise of the Governor's clemency powers." Not one human being out of fifty-four thousand worthy of compassion last year. Not one human being out of fifty-five thousand worthy of compassion this year. Correction: It was granted to one dying man who was to be paroled in four weeks anyway. Either the justice system must be infallible, or the prison system must be a total failure. I wonder why they don't just close the Clemency Bureau and give the money saved to the WIC Program or Head Start or some other place where the money wouldn't be wasted.

Have I ever mentioned that there are presently twenty-two women, in the state of New York, out of over twenty-two hundred, with a lower prison number than I have? That means twenty-two women in the state of New York have served longer in prison on a single charge than I. That makes me one of the .01 percent. Apparently you have befriended one of the most dangerous, evil women in the country. If you should now have second thoughts, I will understand.

The question that frightens me now is how can I fill five more years intelligently and usefully when everything around me screams, "Waste it. That's what it's for. The years are to waste—like the mulberries." I shall do a great deal of knitting—unless they take the yarn away. Perhaps I'll redecorate my cage with a new set of sheets. Perhaps I'll think deep thoughts about the future of capitalism and the everybody-wants-to-be-like-us theory. My compelling infatuation with the concept of the end of history may keep the adrenaline flowing in me. My Fukuyama file now includes a growing library that I'll soon have to send out, since we can have only twenty-five books at a time, including dictionaries; plus two boxes of material on Eastern Europe's and Russia's progress—or lack of it—toward a free market economy, and a box on America's inclination to equate democracy with capitalism.

If I don't make the whole five years, they will find me curled in the fetal position, clutching my Fukuyama file.

Love,
Jean

January 16, 1991

Dear Shana,

Is it possible that the world is at war again? How can it be? We all say how much we hate war, but from everything I hear and read, this is going to be a very popular one . . . and certainly politically correct. I think some members of Congress voted in favor of it because they hadn't the courage of their true convictions. David finds my comments on the subject very tiresome and leaves early if I pursue them.

Strange how nations have such a totally different value scale for individuals than they have for themselves. It brings home to me the present pros and cons about the domestic violence that so many women in here have experienced. When someone in their home batters and beats them, threatens their children, and destroys all hope for a peaceful existence, we ask them, "Why didn't you just move out?" When a nation is thus battered and threatened, it is encouraged to kill the batterer and praised when it does.

Did you notice what happened on Wall Street yesterday? The Dow went up over 100 points. I'm told there's a saying on Wall Street, "Buy on cannons; sell on bells."

Why am I so critical of this little prison? On a national scale it barely exists.

With sadness,
Jean

January 21, 1991

Dear Shana,

It's Sunday and the last day of my week to clean the showers. I hurried out when the doors opened at 6:30 A.M. to get mop and pail and get to work so I'd have the room to myself. I had no sooner started than Pam came barging in with towel and soap and headed for a shower.

"Pam, can't you do that later? I'm trying to clean."

"I gotta take a shower now. I can't go to work without I take a shower."

"When do you have to be at work?"

"Eight o'clock."

"But Pam, it's only six-forty."

"Don't matter. My body gotta have time to *dry*."

I waited until she finished. There are some people you just don't argue with.

Love,
Jean

January 22, 1991

Dear Shana,

At a time when society seems increasingly balkanized by race, sex, education, money, and every conceivable private interest or list of wants, there's a small interesting group of women here who have made a pretty heroic effort to establish an honest-to-God feeling of community. I don't think I've ever mentioned them to you.

"Community" is not a word to bring joy to a prison administrator's heart. To create a working community people have to be empowered to help one another. Prisoners are meant to

176

be impotent. Their keepers are the ones to be empowered. But five years ago a few women concerned about the growing AIDS epidemic formed a group called ACE, acronym for AIDS Counseling and Education. Prisons are the land of drugs, prostitution and every conceivable kind of sexual preference, and consequently of AIDS. I've been told by a member of the medical staff that in a blind test 20 percent of the women here tested positive for the HIV virus. I read someplace else it was 18 percent. Whichever is correct, it's a lot of sick or potentially sick people. AIDS is the main cause of death here. When it burst onto the national scene, no medical facilities were prepared for it, certainly not those in prison. It was a time of panic, disbelief, secrecy, and denial.

In that atmosphere ACE was born, with the stated purposes of trying to reduce high-risk behavior, eliminate the stigmatization of people with AIDS, create a safer and more humane atmosphere for those in the prison, especially in the prison hospital, and build bridges to the outside community so the women would not leave prison with nowhere to go.

Thirty-five women showed up for the first meeting, some with AIDS, others afraid they might have it, and others just interested in learning more about it. The timing was right, and with a good deal of emotion and tentative trust, a few women stood up and said publicly, "I have AIDS." This took guts, since no one had quite decided what policies the prison would adopt toward them. Even now there are jails and prisons where all those who test HIV-positive are kept in separate housing units. That has never happened here.

With the help of a series of lectures by doctors, nurses, and social workers from Montefiore Hospital, some of the women became quite knowledgeable about the disease and ways to counsel and befriend those who have it. They held memorial services for women who died of it, and they adopted the song "Sister" as their theme song. "Lean on me, I am your sister." Their meetings grew larger. Some women volunteered to be on call on a twenty-four-hour basis to go to a sick woman to comfort her, bathe and massage her, keep her company when she was lonely or afraid. And they were allowed to.

All this was with the cooperation and support of the administration. Then suddenly for six months the administration stopped the program. I have no way of knowing all the reasons, but I think they sprang at least in part from a growing discomfort at permitting an inmate group to have so much influence in the prison, and the potential for more. Whatever the reasons, by the end of six months the work they had done was missed and the inmates in ACE were told they could go back to work.

Today ACE women give special birthday parties for AIDS patients and hold bingo games, too. Contributions for prizes are made facilitywide. They've written a puppet show for the children who come to visit their mothers here. They've made their own puppets and even designed and had printed a coloring book for them. Most important, they maintain an ongoing program of education for the new women constantly entering the facility. They've made the inmates aware of themselves as members of a community, of people with common problems who can work together and make a positive difference for one another.

It's sad that it took a national tragedy to jolt many women, certainly not all, into a community, but that's usually what brings people together, isn't it? The remarkable thing is that it has happened at all and been permitted in a top-security prison. I criticize so much that I see here. For this, credit is certainly due, and without administrative support it couldn't have happened.

Jean

February 1, 1991

Dear Shana,

The battle of the bed boards has been brewing for quite some time. As with many battles in here, I find it hard to understand and it frightens me. Senseless things I don't understand and over which I have no control frighten me. I feel as though all the shots being fired are aimed at me, as though I've done something terribly wrong, though logically I know I haven't.

Some women here need bed boards. I am one of them, having had a history of a bad back before I arrived here; in fact, I've even worn a heavy corset for support at various times. I have had a bed board for nine years, with the doctor's initialed permission on a special yellow slip, which I can find at some times and can't find at others. Until recently, nurses were permitted to update the permission annually. Now, each year each inmate must make a doctor's appointment, going first through Nurses' Screening to get the appointment and then getting the doctor's permission. I find it poor use of a doctor's time, but nobody asked me. Recently, one of the nurses sounded the alarm that there were women in this prison who had bed boards without proper permission. She called the floors and told the COs to check every bed and if the inmate couldn't produce the written permission, we were told to "Give back the board. Give it back. Right now. Take it off the bed." I can't lift the mattress, let alone the bed board. After much shouting and leaving my heart down where my stomach used to be, the CO calmed down and seemed to forget how terribly important the whole thing was, so I left the bed board where it was and signed up for Nurses' Screening to start the road to the doctor. I was lucky. The doctor gave me permission. Some with equal need weren't as lucky. Giving no reason at all, one doctor in particular just said no.

I'm told the cause of this excitement is that some women

179

have been known to break up their bed boards to build a shelf. Shelves are not permitted in cells. Some women have even been known to break up a bed board just for the hell of it, or because they're angry. Obviously, those are the ones who will not be asking for permission to continue using a board. They will be asking for a new one. It shouldn't be too hard to check this out. It also shouldn't be hard to figure out, after a woman has been sleeping on a bed board for nine years, whether she's using it properly or building shelves.

I will never, never grow accustomed to being considered a liar and a cheat and being treated like one every day. A whole lifetime to the contrary is as nothing. It's a strange psychological approach for people who persist in labeling their work as "correctional." It's also a strange approach in a state that needs to put all its people, including doctors, and all its money to the best possible use.

Everything I tried and succeeded in accomplishing as a mother and as a teacher was built on an atmosphere of trust. Everything here shrieks "folly" to that. I find it impossible to put into words what mental agony that is for me, the control it takes sometimes to keep from screaming. Imagine living a whole life like this. Imagine wanting to work under such conditions.

Jean

February 5, 1991

Dear Shana,

A woman in Detroit has just written to tell me, "I am in possession of a copy of the magazine *High Heels*, dated January 1938. I have reason to believe that some of the photographs in the magazine are of you. Would you care to comment?"

I guess the kindest thing to do is choose not to comment. Better to save that air of mystery that should, by rights, hang over every notorious woman. I always tell too much. Was Jeannie Baby at age fifteen leading a double life, conjugating her verbs on Monday, slipping off to pose for girlie magazines on Thursday? Who knows? The Shadow knows.

Love,
Tootsie

February 12, 1991

Dear Shana,

If I could relive any part of my life, I would ask for the first year of their lives with each of my sons. Not that I didn't love them enough the first time around but because this time around I could appreciate more the marvel of their accomplishments. I would look at them with new eyes. I would congratulate them more. I wouldn't take for granted the first time they purposely clapped two hands together instead of waving them randomly in the air. And I would know they were on the intellectual high road when the rattle fell and they looked down to see where it had gone. Did you know that is one of the giant steps in human intellectual development? It means you've grown beyond the total egocentrism of a newborn infant. You no longer think things cease to exist if you can't see them. You know they're somewhere else but they still exist, and you wonder about them enough to look for them. In short, you can now play peekaboo and hide-and-seek.

If one could stretch the truth enough to say it's possible to find a source of pleasure in prison, I have found it in my reading about and observing of infants. It has opened up for me a whole new piece of the world—a totally new awareness

181

and an awesome respect for the miracle of life as a healthy infant lives it.

The importance of eye contact is what gives me my greatest pangs of conscience. I'd hate to tell you how many books I read during those 2:00 A.M. feedings. Like so many other mothers, I'm afraid, I thought what the child wanted was the milk. Which they do, of course, but they also want a little sociability and conversation over dinner. Don't we all? Eyes do much of the talking to a baby. My sons were raised with a mixture of eyes and the side of my head, and an occasional bump when I rearranged them for a minute while I turned a page. They've survived, all right, but I think we all missed something.

I think seriously of writing a book about the miracle of infancy, the miracle of first learnings and all the important ways parents can play a role in it. But then I pull back, wondering how many people would say, "Who the hell is she to tell me how to raise my kid?" It would be a personal risk. Just about everything useful is, but I'm not quite sure I feel strong enough to take it. Later, perhaps. On second thought, this is about as late as it's going to get.

Love,
Jean

EPILOGUE

February 28, 1991

Dear Shana,

If my memory serves me, and it doesn't very well, today marks the anniversary of my tenth year in prison. I could find out for sure by lying on my stomach and squirming under my bed to the farthest corner and pulling out the box that holds some of my legal papers, but knowing isn't that important to me. It's ten years, give or take a day. Don't send flowers or have a tray engraved. As a matter of fact, I can't remember anymore whether my wedding anniversary was the twenty-fifth or twenty-sixth of May, but that doesn't matter much either.

The worst thing about anniversaries is that they tend to make one nostalgic, or worse still, philosophical, two things much to be avoided, especially in prison. You find yourself asking, "Well, what did you expect life to be? Did you think it would be a rose garden? Did you bother to think at all?" That last question is the hard one. The truth is, I didn't think much about the whole thing, just did my Girl Scout best each day, which I have discovered late is a thoroughly inadequate preparation for life.

I've heard life referred to as a vale of tears, which I don't

183

like at all. I heard Malcolm Muggeridge say, "Life in this world is like a night in a second-class hotel." That impressed me as terribly sophisticated at the time, and it does leave room for a couple of good laughs, but it doesn't fill the bill either.

In here, God knows, life is not a rose garden. "It's not supposed to be," you hear the crowd shouting. Nothing lovely flourishes here. Little that is good is nourished here. What grows here is hypocrisy, obscenity, illness, illegality, ignorance, confusion, waste, hopelessness. Life in prison is a garden of dross, cultivated by those who never check to see what their crop is. Ten years in a garden of dross! So, as the poet said, you plant your own garden and cultivate your own soul. Maybe that's what life is.

I don't know. That second-class hotel doesn't sound too bad.

Love,
Jean

INDEX

About the Author

JEAN HARRIS, born in Chicago, Illinois, was educated at Smith College. She spent several decades as a teacher and administrator before she became headmistress of the Madeira School in McLean, Virginia. A fifteen-year relationship with Dr. Herman Tarnower ended tragically, with Tarnower's death. Despite her denials, Jean Harris was convicted of second-degree murder. She is now serving her sentence at the Bedford Hills Correctional Facility.